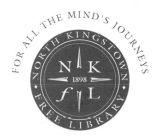

FOR ALL THE MIND'S JOURNEYS

NORTH KINGSTOWN

N K

1898

f L

FREE LIBRARY

In Memoriam

Thomas E. Steere III

Hidden Witness

HIDDEN

ST. MARTIN'S PRESS

NEW YORK

WITNESS

AFRICAN-AMERICAN IMAGES *from the* DAWN *of* PHOTOGRAPHY *to the* CIVIL WAR

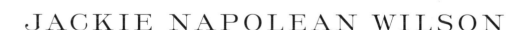

JACKIE NAPOLEAN WILSON

This book is based on the exhibition

HIDDEN WITNESS: AFRICAN-AMERICANS IN EARLY PHOTOGRAPHY

(February 28–June 18, 1995, at the J. Paul Getty Museum, Malibu, California).

For information address St. Martin's Press, 175 Fifth Avenue, New York, N.Y. 10010.

Printed in Hong Kong

BOOK DESIGN *by* HENRY SENE YEE / HOT MONKEY DeSIGN • *Design Assistant:* VICTORIA KUSKOWSKI

Library of Congress Cataloging-in-Publication Data

Wilson, Jackie Napolean.
    Hidden Witness: African-American images from the dawn of
photography to the Civil War / Jackie Napolean Wilson.—1st ed.
       p. cm.
    ISBN 0-312-24546-7
     1. Portrait photography—United States—History—19th century.
2. Afro-Americans portraits. 3. Slaves—United States Portraits.
I. Title.
TR680.W55   1999
779'.9973'0496073—dc21   99-15938
                                   CIP

FIRST EDITION: OCTOBER 1999

10 9 8 7 6 5 4 3 2 1

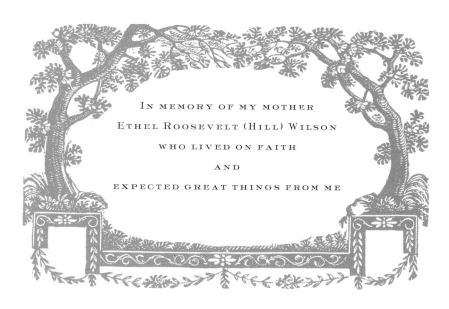

In memory of my mother
Ethel Roosevelt (Hill) Wilson
who lived on faith
and
expected great things from me

FOREWORD

COLLECTING IS SOMETHING PEOPLE DO FOR reasons buried deep inside themselves. To be a good collector requires a big heart, an open mind, and lots of faith because the collector will inevitably find himself taken to unexpected places. Trained as a lawyer, but in spirit a poet and painter, Jackie Napolean Wilson, like many acquisitors, is a man of depth and contradiction. His collection of photographs of African-Americans around the time of the abolition of slavery is, for him, a door that opens the creative process. The texts he has written to accompany the images in this book spring simultaneously from emotion and analysis. Not long after Jackie and I first met in Detroit in 1992, when we got to know each other in his gracious Arts and Crafts—style home filled with a great variety of artifacts pertaining to people of African descent in America, I invited him to come to Los Angeles, to study the Getty Museum's holding of photographs depicting African-Americans at the middle of the last century. While he was in Los Angeles, Jackie discovered a dozen or so important photographs in the Getty collection that had never before been recognized as having a connection to African-American history. Our conversations covered many topics. We discovered how complementary the Getty and Wilson collections are, with the Wilson collection strong in vernacular subjects and the Getty strong in material of historical importance. We shared astonishment at how a photograph can so vividly reveal the very look in a person's eyes, the shapes of their ears, how they groomed their hair, what type of clothes they wore, how they stood as well as further intangible messages transmitted through body language. Considering the potential interest and importance of the subject of African-Americans around the time of the abolition of slavery, we wondered why there had never been an exhibition or book devoted to portraits of black people in the middle of the last century. ❧ One reason is that such pictures are very rare to begin with—there were very few African-American photographers and very few black people had the money, time, or freedom for a portrait sitting—and those pictures that do exist are not well documented as to maker, place, subject, or date. Moreover, they are widely dispersed in local historical societies and private collections, rather than in the major urban museums of art and history. The Getty Museum, for example, holds a collection of some fifteen hundred daguerreotypes, ambrotypes, and tintypes, yet there are only thirty such images, which experts consider a large holding. ❧ Jackie Napolean Wilson has earned a place in history by discovering in our collection the wonderful picture, *A Family Seated in its Garden,* giving to it the title *Hidden Witness,* as it was displayed in the exhibition of the same name. Jackie also saw the inner beauty and outer beauty of the unknown mother and child (the concluding plate in his book). If he were only responsible for preserving this picture alone, the world would still owe him a very large debt of gratitude.

—WESTON NAEF, *Los Angeles, April 1999*

INTRODUCTION

MY GRANDFATHER WAS BORN A SLAVE ON A plantation in Spartanburg, South Carolina, between 1853 and 1855 (the exact date is unknown because the birthdays of slaves were not recorded). He often said he was between ten and twelve years old when the Civil War ended. His father served as a Negro camp cook during the Civil War, from 1861 to 1865, under General Stonewall Jackson in the Kershaw's Brigade in the Confederate army. He traveled on to Harpers Ferry, to the great land battles, to the battlefield at Gettysburg, and to the close of the war.   Before the Civil War, in 1860, the population of Americans of African descent was 4.5 million, about four-fifths of whom were slaves located mostly in the South. The Republic and public opinion tended to hold a deep-seated, vehement, and unrelenting preju-dice against the colored races throughout the country, which barred equal civil and political rights. Many churches also tended to lend themselves to this bitterness toward a people.   Amid these circumstances, the light of photography was introduced in 1839, a time when the art of picture-taking was scarcely available to African-Americans. Those who were free were marginally better than slaves themselves, save for those who somehow overcame and rose above their plight. Initially, free blacks worked in daguerreotypy, but historically the slave and free black primarily served the dominant race and were not often sitters in photographs. Early African-American photographers such as Jules Lyon of New

The man's body is sacred, and the woman's body is sacred. No matter who it is—it is sacred...

—WALT WHITMAN

Orleans, Augustus Washington of New England (who expatriated to Liberia), and James P. Ball from Cincinnati were among the first daguerreotypists in America and their patronage was nearly exclusively white. Besides the expense of a photograph, social and legal restrictions limited the accessibility of this profound invention among those of African descent, slave and free. ❧ Nearly all histories of the antebellum period and the American Civil War era have relied upon a small number of woodcuts and an even smaller number of photographs to illustrate the condition and appearance of African-Americans, but this body of visual images was fostered and remains marred with the apparent biases of the painters, printmakers, and publishers who created and issued them. ❧ Even so, these often anonymous photographers left a mirror, focusing distant light on a past that touched African-Americans throughout the country. Pictures of the slave are rare, and of the free black scant during this period. These photographs, then, are the nearest glimpse of what these enslaved and marginally free Americans looked like from the dawning of photography in America to the end of American slavery. These are real people as they may have appeared to Jefferson Davis, Frederick A. Douglass, Robert E. Lee, Abraham Lincoln, Charles S. Sumner, Sojourner Truth, friends and foes to the cause of freedom. ❧ Photography was most certainly used to portray this period and to justify, explain, and record this conflict that changed the world. But if one were to make a visual photographic assessment of America at that time, one might ponder where the subjects of this great conflict were. Visually, African-Americans are seldom depicted in history books. The historical record has been lost in many instances, but there can be extracted an interpretation of the actors when viewing these photographs. Census records show that Negroes lived on both sides of the Mason-Dixon line. How, then, did they appear?

—JACKIE NAPOLEAN WILSON, *Detroit, April 1999*

A NOTE TO THE READER

PHOTOGRAPHY FIRST CAME TO AMERICA IN THE FORM OF THE daguerreotype in the spring of 1839, not long after its first appearance in Paris earlier in the year. Light-sensitive silver was at the heart of most early photographic processes, and the daguerreotype was created on a sheet of copper that had been electrolytically plated with silver. The silvered copper plate was sensitized by exposing it to light, and then developed with vapors of mercury. The finished picture, magically trapped on the mirrorlike surface, was preserved in a hinged case made of wood and leather or other craft materials. Very few American photographic images of any subject survive from before about 1845 to 1855, when the daguerreotype was replaced by a cheaper and easier method, the ambrotype. An ambrotype was made by adhering the light-sensitive silver salts to a glass plate with a very sticky substance, then exposing it in a wooden camera with a large brass lens similar to the kind used for making a daguerreotype. Ambrotypes were presented in three-dimensional cases similar to daguerreotypes. The ambrotype process was replaced by the tintype around 1859. A tintype was made by adhering the light-sensitive materials to a piece of tin. Ambrotypes and tintypes could be made with shorter exposures and less light than daguerreotypes, and with less complicated chemistry to finish the process. Ambrotypes and tintypes proliferated because they were less time consuming to make and used less expensive materials, costing the sitter less money. The sizes of the daguerreotypes reproduced here are given using the traditional terminology from the daguerreian era. Within each category, the actual sizes of the plates vary slightly from image to image:

WHOLE PLATE	8 1/2 X 6 1/2 INCHES
THREE-QUARTER PLATE	7 1/8 X 5 1/2 INCHES
HALF PLATE	5 1/2 X 4 1/2 INCHES
QUARTER PLATE	4 1/4 X 3 1/4 INCHES
SIXTH PLATE	3 1/4 X 2 3/4 INCHES
NINTH PLATE	2 1/2 X 2 INCHES

HIDDEN WITNESS

CHARLES H. FONTAYNE AND WILLIAM SOUTHGATE PORTER

American, active Cincinnati, 1848–53

Family in Garden ("The Hidden Witness"), ca. 1853

THREE-QUARTER PLATE DAGUERREOTYPE
84.XT.269.7

THE J. PAUL GETTY MUSEUM, LOS ANGELES

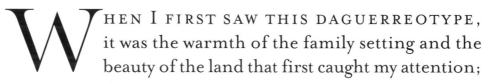

WHEN I FIRST SAW THIS DAGUERREOTYPE, it was the warmth of the family setting and the beauty of the land that first caught my attention;

later I saw this man forlorn with shovel in hand leaning against the tree and knew that this was a memorial planting in the garden of a park of a Greek Revival home. I also saw a woman peering from the back porch as though she were an indentured servant. This daguerreotype was likely made in the South. However, the maker's mark is in Cincinnati, Ohio.

This slave gardener made the scene himself. He was the "hidden witness" who saw this picture being created and was a witness to life at that time, and remained a testimonial to this day. This was a daydream picture. It appears he thought he was out of reach while watching these people who seemed to have everything and wondering what life would be like if he were in their place. I wonder what happened when they saw this picture with him in it when he should have been working.

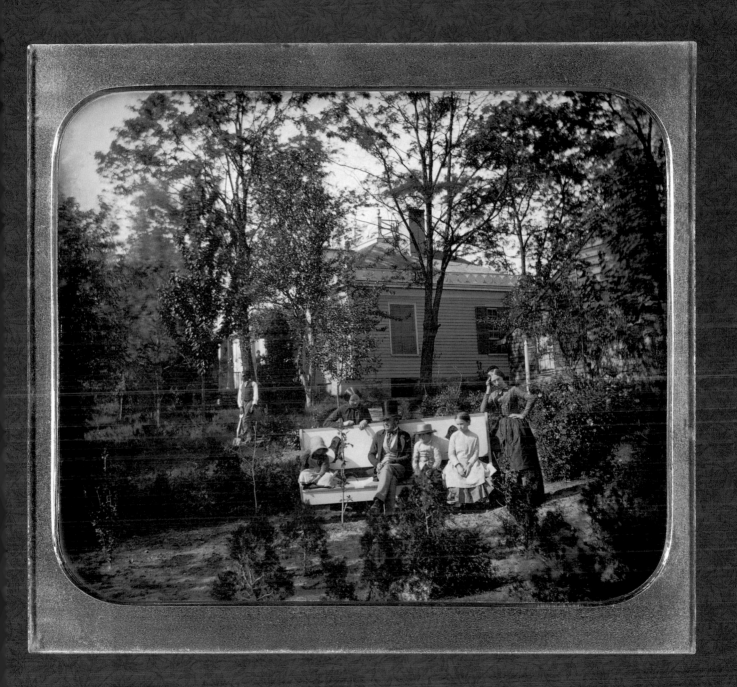

UNKNOWN MAKER

American School

A Window into Time, ca. 1860

SIXTH-PLATE AMBROTYPE

JACKIE NAPOLEAN WILSON COLLECTION

Henry Whiting's store built in 1852 and burned in April 1911. Not a brick left standing.
—NOTE ON BACK OF IMAGE WRITTEN IN BROWN INK

AFRICANS WERE NOT BROUGHT TO THESE shores for city living. They were meant for heavy labor and for the work of servants to maintain other people's comfort in agricultural settings. But along with the country's historical progression, the slaves also graduated from the frontier and life on the plantation to the county and the town. African-Americans born free, freed, or who bought their freedom were still not equal to whites, their status being little better than slaves. This scenario, suspended in time, is one of the earliest stop-action images in commerce. There is no way to know whether these persons were free or slaves. Some slaves were permitted to hire out their own time, to move about with restrictions; and they typically lived on the owner's lot or lived elsewhere with certain conditions. The free black was a threat to slavery and through custom and law was restricted to certain occupations, regulated group gatherings, and curfew. Laws were enacted to require free blacks to post bond or leave the state.

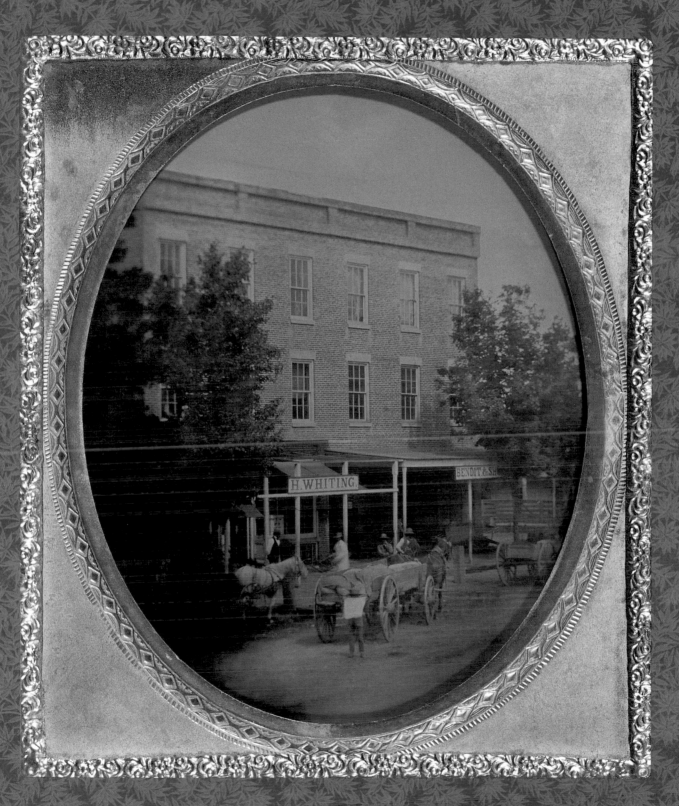

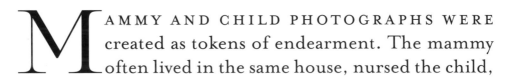

MAMMY AND CHILD PHOTOGRAPHS WERE created as tokens of endearment. The mammy often lived in the same house, nursed the child, and cared for it for many years as part of the family. Since there was no legal or religious recognition of slave marriages, slaves were denied conventional families, and their children could be taken from them and sold, and for some slaves the children of their masters were treated as though their own.

In a legal sense, the child was the owner and the woman was its property. The child is the subject of this photograph and the woman is present to keep the child in position for the photographer. She tenderly caresses the child, with her head modestly directed away from the camera, by way of acknowledging that her face is not essential to this portrait.

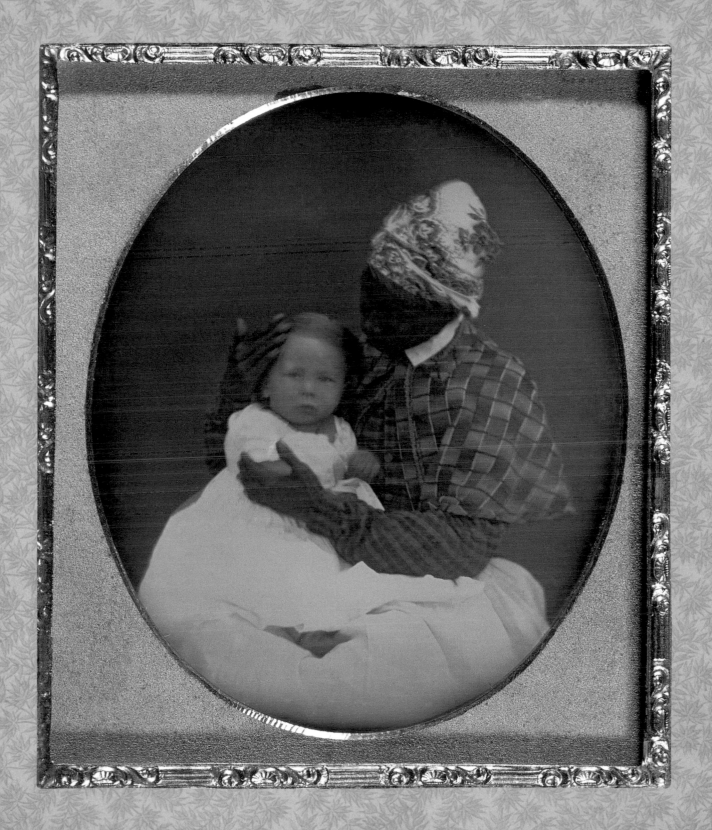

UNKNOWN MAKER

American School

Portrait of a Nurse and Young Child, ca. 1850

SIXTH-PLATE DAGUERREOTYPE

84.XT.172.4

THE J. PAUL GETTY MUSEUM, LOS ANGELES

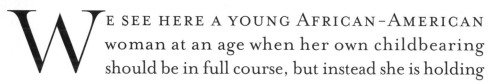

W E SEE HERE A YOUNG AFRICAN-AMERICAN woman at an age when her own childbearing should be in full course, but instead she is holding another woman's child. Her rounded cheeks and full face suggest girth, and she gives the impression of strong support to the householder's loved one. What a sadness of toil in her eyes, what a large hand with large fingers holding the child toward the world. Her splayed fingers lovingly cradle her charge. Her head covering was proscribed by law and entrenched as custom in parts of the South.

Where was the real mother during this photography session, in those days an important event in a child's life? There is a certain sadness in the eyes of the "mammy." Her fingers—strong, yet tender—are notable; yet her face is asymmetrical, one side showing calm melancholy and the other suggesting some distress.

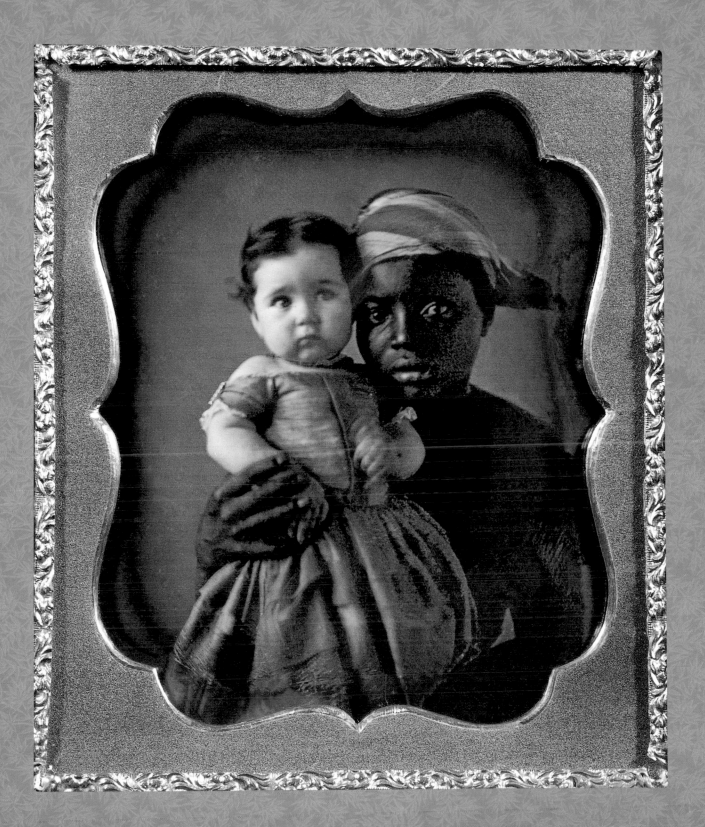

IT WAS NOT THE PHOTOGRAPHER WHO CAUSED this mammy to appear as a statuesque Nubian princess; it was her birthright, though she was born a slave. It is remarkable that she wears no scarf or head rag. She may have been her mistress's trusted confidante. Some slaves were able to receive jewelry from the mistress. Her good taste in dress, earrings, and jeweled brooch, along with the size of the daguerreotype, suggest owners of opulence who, perhaps, allowed her some freedoms in slavery.

Though the eyes in most "mammy and child" portraits show strength, sadness, and survival, there is also emotion and resignation in these pictures. Could it be that these slave women's feelings evolved because they knew the child would not be taken away as children of slaves sometimes were? Did this responsibility provide a form of protection and security that would also allow the slave to explore emotions that were not bestowed upon her own children? Maybe there was no emotional involvement between the mammy and her charge, and instead we see a woman who is simply obedient to the slave culture into which she was born, and who wears a mask of affection that was part of the job.

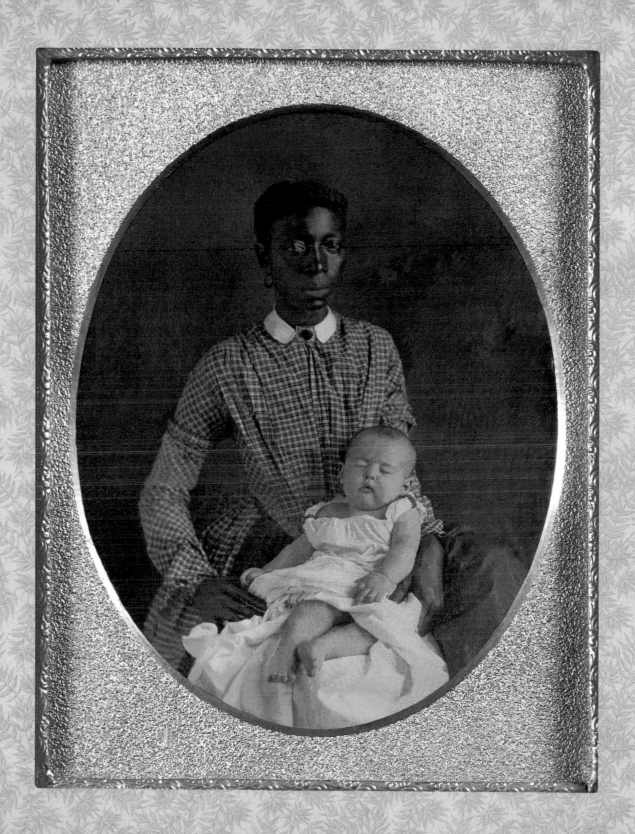

UNKNOWN MAKER

American School

Mother and Daughter, ca. 1860

SIXTH-PLATE AMBROTYPE

JACKIE WILSON NAPOLEAN COLLECTION

AFRICAN-AMERICAN GIRLS ARE NOT OFTEN seen in historical photography, even less so than boys. In this picture, the mother does not have much likeness to the daughter or stepdaughter. She seems mulatto. Both subjects are well dressed. The father probably traveled much and this ambrotype was given to him as keepsake. This was no doubt a well-to-do Negro woman for her time, and probably a woman of stature in her community. The face of the girl is intense, but there is no close attachment shown between this mother and daughter. Perhaps they left their community to have this picture taken and the child conceals their relation for the photographer.

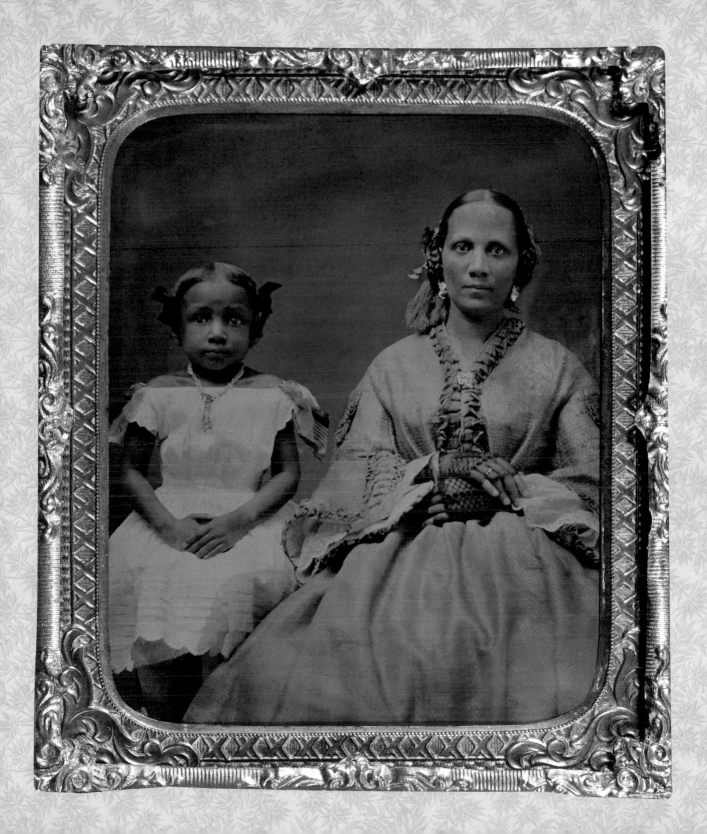

THOMAS MARTIN EASTERLY

American, 1809–1882

Portrait of a Father, Daughters, and Nurse, ca. 1850

QUARTER-PLATE DAGUERREOTYPE

84. XT.1569.1

THE J. PAUL GETTY MUSEUM, LOS ANGELES

WE SEE THIS COMMISSIONED ARTIST'S boldness of light, his sympathetic modeling of his subjects; but the completeness of the conception must not overshadow the plain truth. To instill this trust, this slave mammy was separated from the slave quarters, her life was molded by the dominant society and she shared and appeased their intimacies. And this slave woman appears to have ruled the roost. Given her demeanor and her age, she may have been this slaveholder's mammy, too; and was now mammy to his daughters, continuing on alone in the wake of the mistress's death. But, under all circumstances, she was still a slave from cradle to grave; but her strength cannot be masked, not even by a master in the art of photography.

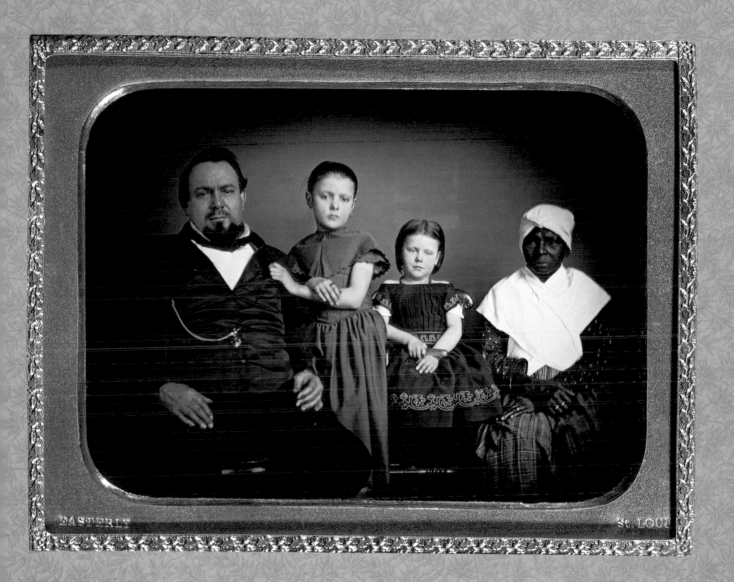

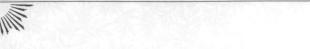

16

THIS IS A SOUTHERN URBAN townhouse typical of Charleston, South Carolina, and it illustrates the cultural separation between the races. It is undeniably Southern, with slaves on a separate plane even though all lived in the same household. This is the city where Denmark Vesey, an ex-slave, conspired against slavery in 1822. Lincoln and Douglas debated the slavery issue here in 1858. The city contained the largest population of free blacks in the South and many slaves engaged in commerce in numerous occupations, hiring themselves out for their masters' gain. And, on a small island, near to the entrance to this city, is Fort Sumter where the Civil War commenced.

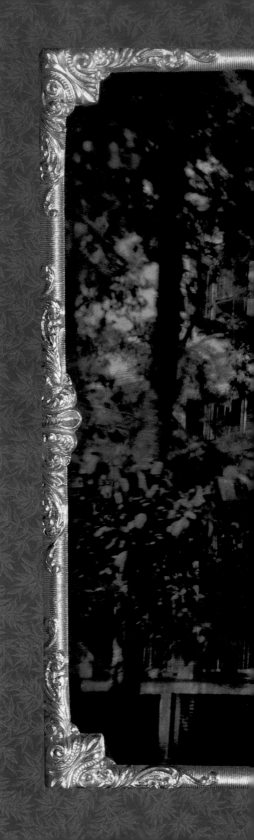

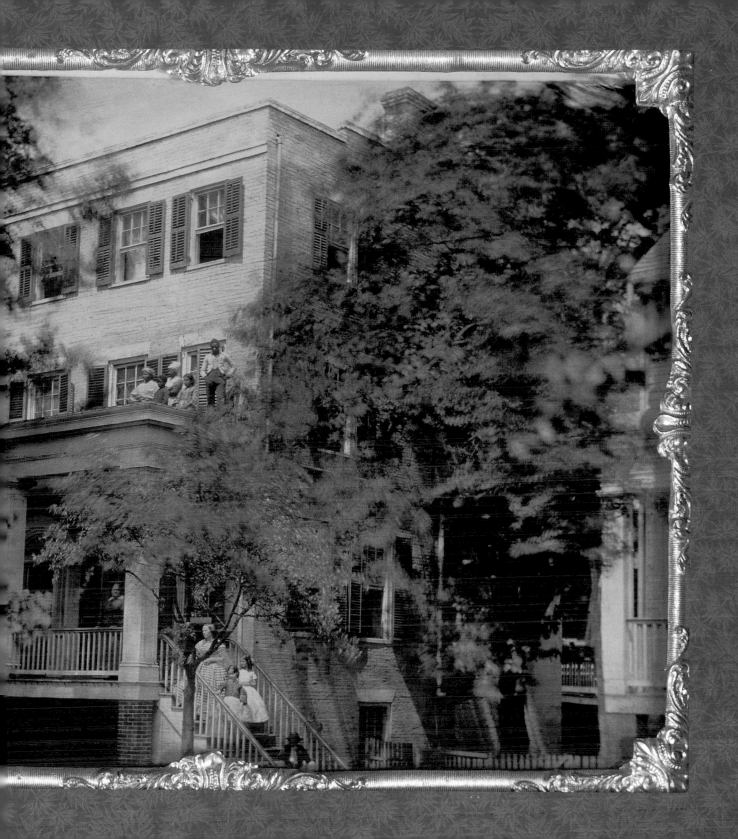

UNKNOWN MAKER

American School

Group Portrait in a Kitchen Garden, ca. 1860

SIXTH-PLATE AMBROTYPE

JACKIE NAPOLEAN WILSON COLLECTION

THIS IS A SOUTHERN KITCHEN GARDEN photographed from high ground, likely the back veranda of the plantation. The garden with its rows of vegetables and flowers and its water pump is just outside of the kitchen. The household staff portrayed consists of a cook, a personal maid, and a body servant, in the company of a young man and three young girls—children of the master. Perhaps all are children of the master, save for the cook, who could have been the mother of the two mulatto slaves. With this much detail, this is too small and intimate a photograph to be displayed. Its nature is that of a keepsake for personal and private recollection.

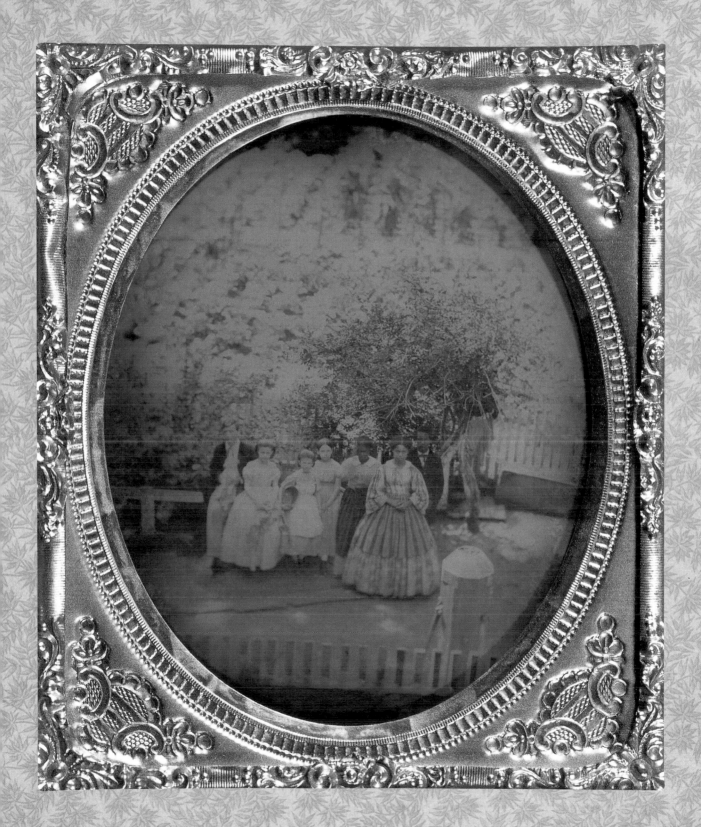

UNKNOWN MAKER

American School

The Wedding Scene, ca. 1860

HALF-PLATE TINTYPE

JACKIE NAPOLEAN WILSON COLLECTION

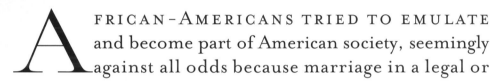

AFRICAN-AMERICANS TRIED TO EMULATE and become part of American society, seemingly against all odds because marriage in a legal or religious sense was denied to slaves. This is the earliest known photograph of a free African-American wedding scene before the Civil War. In the South, marriage between two slaves was illegal, and this event may have taken place in a border state or in the North.

Many slaveholders denied marriage to their slaves. Some allowed only a temporary union by selection, by consent, or by the proverbial method of jumping over the broomstick. A few permitted it by religious ceremony, but most barred marriage by their slaves altogether. Marriage would have interfered with the economic structure of the slave economy, creating problems such as family separations, inheritance, and slave breeding. To allow the sacrament of marriage would have given slaves a sense of integrity, and would have created an undesired sense of heritage and family history. But this group portrait is of free people seeming to herald a gift of God and nature.

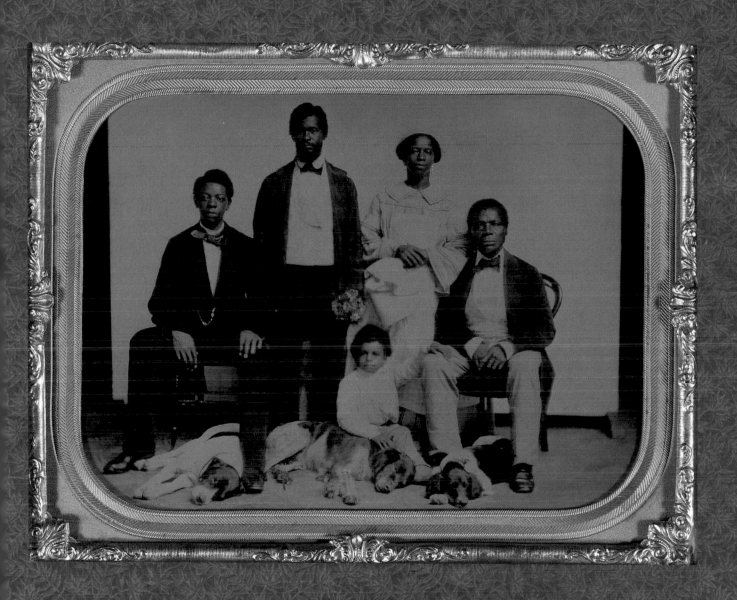

UNKNOWN MAKER

American School

Fireman and Bride, ca. 1860

QUARTER-PLATE TINTYPE

JACKIE NAPOLEAN WILSON COLLECTION

THIS WOMAN SEEMS TIMID AND SHY, BUT the man is confident and poised in what seems a wedding photograph. He is in a fireman's uniform, and wears a Zouave braided jacket and white gloves. He must have had another occupation for livelihood, as firefighting was a civic duty at that time. He holds her hand in his white-gloved right hand and she holds her white hat with flowing ribbon in her other hand. At the periphery are some telling symbols: a thick book, perhaps a Bible, on the wooden post and a tintype case on top of the book. The painted backdrop and the rustic props suggest that this tintype was taken outdoors.

Although this man and woman may appear perfectly natural and assimilated into a free society, they lived at a time when the boundaries between races were clearly defined.

Before the Emancipation Proclamation was signed into law, every African-American had to prove on demand that they were legally free. This couple had every reason to be nervous or unsettled because the laws favored white people. Did they have to distance themselves from their enslaved brethren? Did they exhibit in their lifestyle and appearance any sympathy toward the free, impoverished Negro and the enslaved?

Because being married and raising a family were rights enjoyed by only a small number of African-Americans in the middle of the last century, very few people today have portraits of their ancestors prior to 1865.

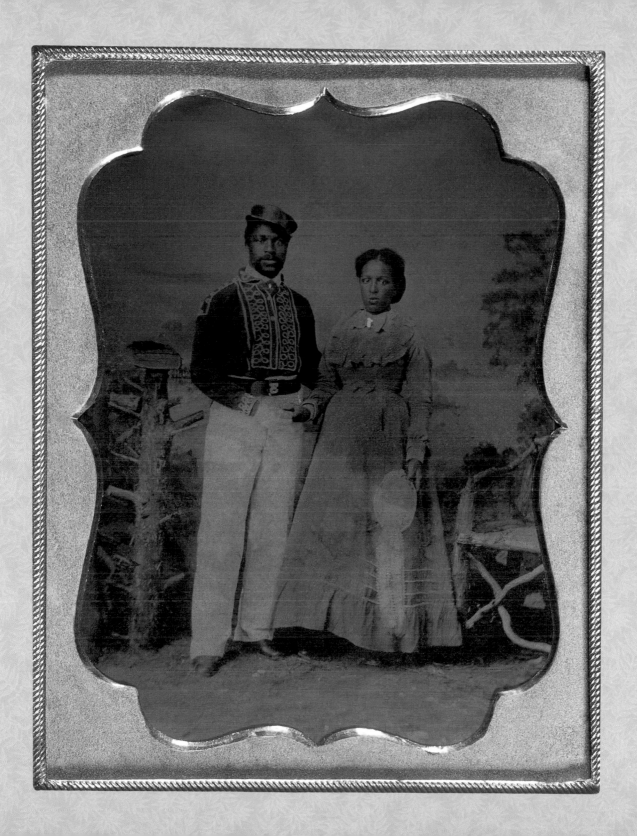

UNKNOWN MAKER

American School

Sisters Holding Hands, ca. 1845

QUARTER-PLATE DAGUERREOTYPE

JACKIE NAPOLEAN WILSON COLLECTION

THESE TWO MULATTO WOMEN WERE LIKELY sisters. The tender handholding and the cradling of fans are gestures that may have been spontaneous or may have been orchestrated by the photographer. Judging by their faces and their composure, these young African-American women appear familiar with the comforts of life. Only a very small number of African-Americans reached this level of prosperity in the nineteenth century. In order for the subjects to appear more natural, daguerreotypes were often carefully hand-colored, as is the case here.

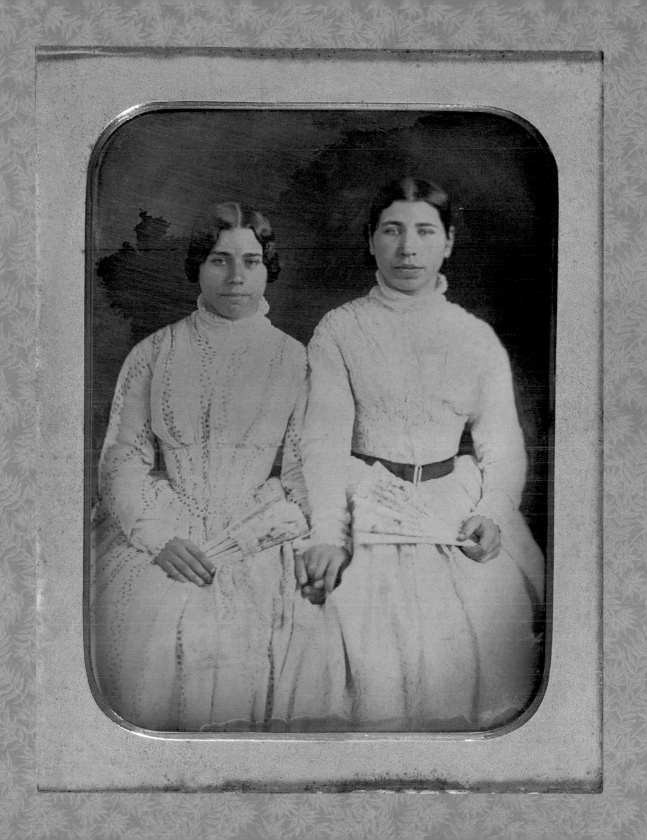

UNKNOWN MAKER

American School

"Life of the Cause," Woman Abolitionists, ca. 1855

SIXTH-PLATE DAGUERREOTYPE

JACKIE NAPOLEAN WILSON COLLECTION

THESE TWO WOMEN ARE SIMILARLY DRESSED, the child's affectation is jointly shared. More women were sympathetic with the abolition of slavery than were men; William Lloyd Garrison, a fervent abolitionist, believed that women were "the life of the cause." Slavery, inequality, and male dominance brought many women together in the antislavery societies from the 1830s onward. Very often abolitionists sought to remove the stain of slavery from the land, but they did not always believe that abolition would mean there should be equality between the races. And not all abolitionist societies welcomed free blacks to participate with them in the cause. Here we see expressed an unusual example of social equality between a black and white woman.

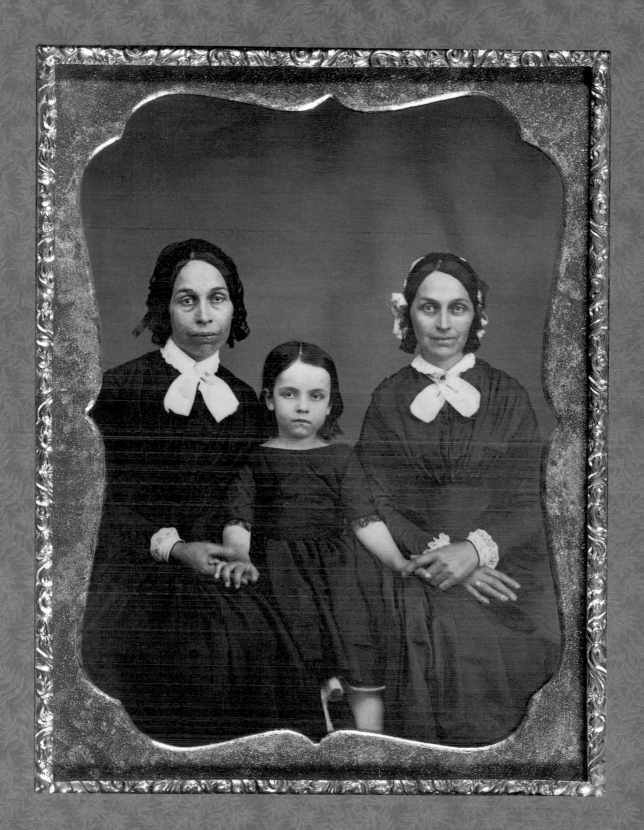

UNKNOWN MAKER

American School

Three-Story House with Classical Porch, ca. 1851

HALF-PLATE DAGUERREOTYPE

84.XT.441.24

THE J. PAUL GETTY MUSEUM, LOS ANGELES

28

A PROFESSIONAL PHOTOGRAPHER would have been summoned to this Southern city residence to capture this occasion. The male servants, in high top hats and frock coats, were on duty as attendants for the arrival of guests. They were to be escorted to the madam standing at the door. Throughout the antebellum era, Americans were influenced by the British in dress, custom, and protocol, but not in the manner of slavery—slavery having no precedent under English law. Male servants were separated from their families, hindered from forming their own families, and were required to live on their owner's premises. Some slave owners threatened to send servants back to the field as field hands.

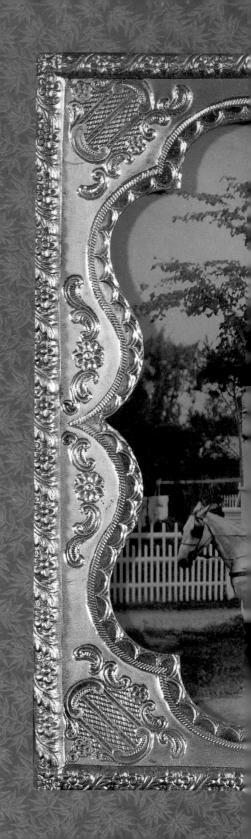

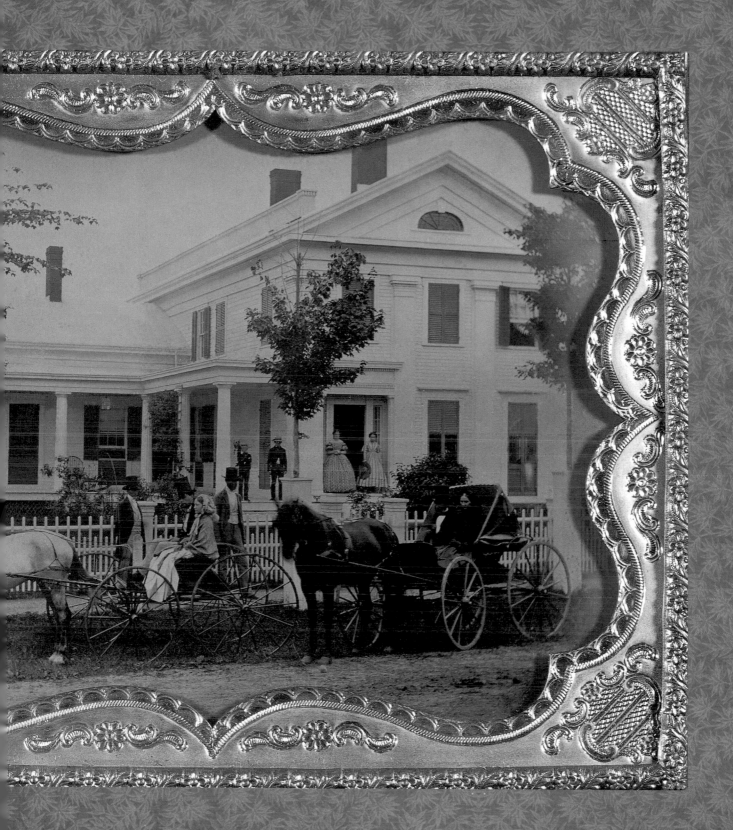

UNKNOWN MAKER

American School

Grist Mill, ca. 1845

SIXTH-PLATE DAGUERREOTYPE
84.XT.1581.8

THE J. PAUL GETTY MUSEUM, LOS ANGELES

THE NATURAL CAREER OF slavery was in agriculture. This slave owner had a capably managed plantation. This is a rarely seen grouping of free white hires and slaves, an arrangement that occurred on many plantations. Shown is a close relationship between free and slave labor. Many rural whites found themselves in poverty and "hired out" on plantations, along with skilled workmen.

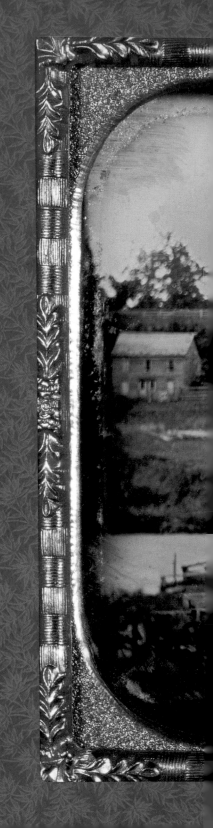

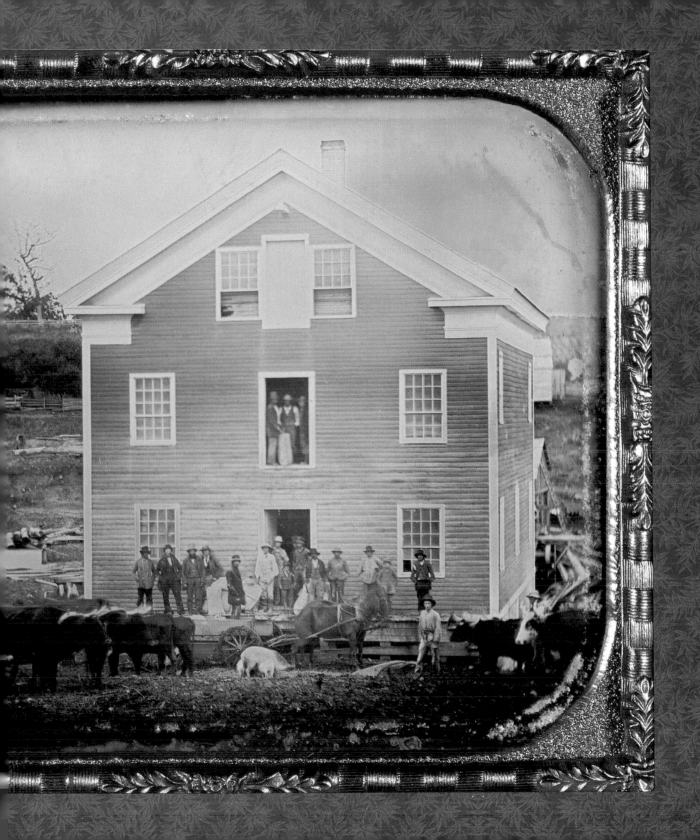

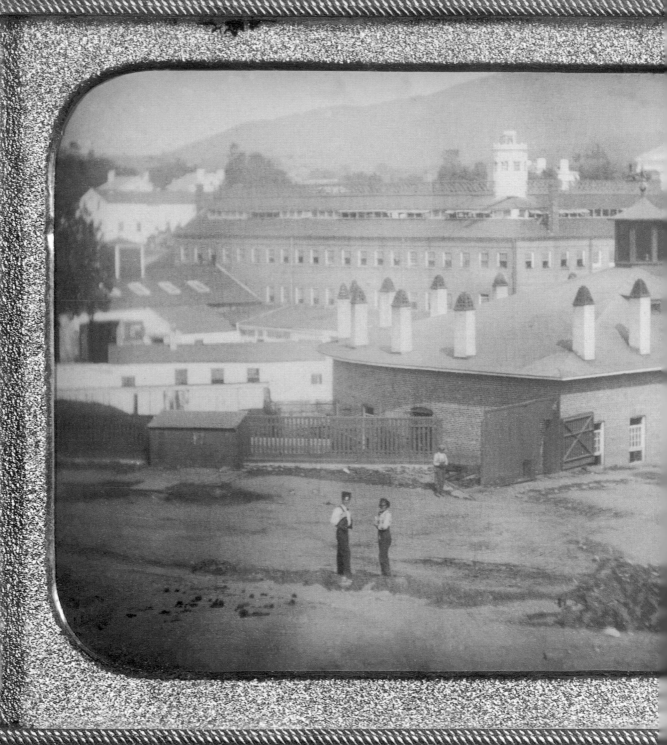

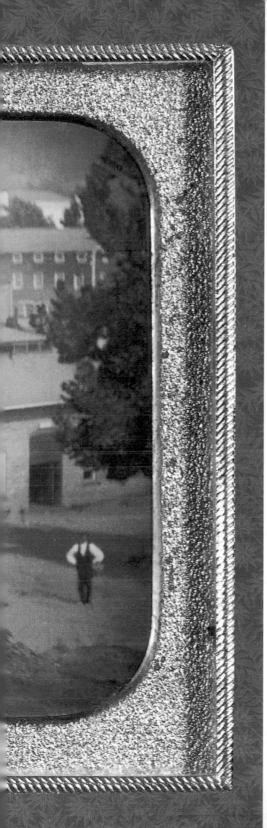

UNKNOWN MAKER

American School

Auburn State Prison, Auburn, New York, ca. 1850

QUARTER-PLATE DAGUERREOTYPE

84.XT.1581.9

THE J. PAUL GETTY MUSEUM, LOS ANGELES

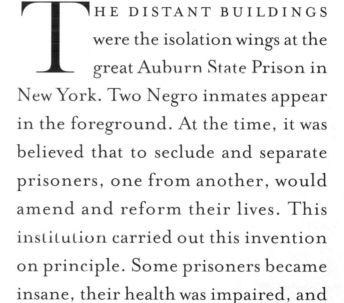

THE DISTANT BUILDINGS were the isolation wings at the great Auburn State Prison in New York. Two Negro inmates appear in the foreground. At the time, it was believed that to seclude and separate prisoners, one from another, would amend and reform their lives. This institution carried out this invention on principle. Some prisoners became insane, their health was impaired, and life was endangered.

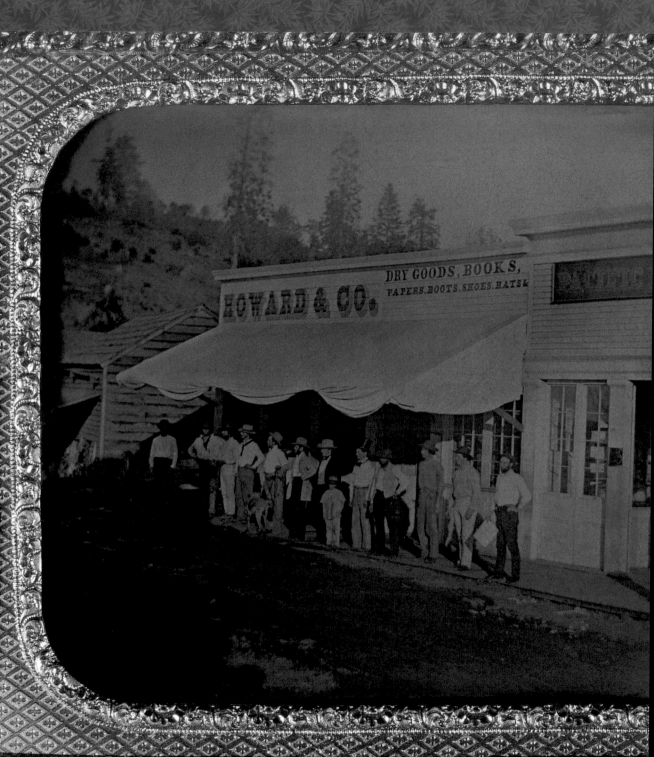

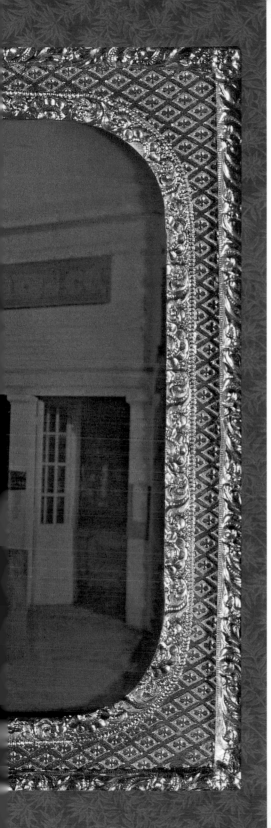

UNKNOWN MAKER

American School

Rough and Ready Mining Camp, California, 1855

SIXTH-PLATE AMBROTYPE
84.XT.1589.15

THE J. PAUL GETTY MUSEUM, LOS ANGELES

P EOPLE CAME FROM ALL OVER THE world to the gold mining foothills of California. The man in the high top hat must have brought the boy along on the trip. The Negro stands next to this man. California was a free state when this ambrotype was taken, but the political issue of pro-slavery or freedom was not settled until 1860. There was even discussion about dividing California into two states, the southern half delivered over to slavery. ❧ The photographer's work is like an artifact from a town's archaeological excavation. This image is a primary source of how people were positioned according to social or political values of the time. Several have hands on their hips with the candid immediacy of the shadow before them, which seems to be machinery. Outside the Pacific Express Company, the man holding the front page of a newspaper holds a record of some event related to the subjects in the ambrotype.

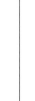

UNKNOWN MAKER

American School

J. Silsby Stage House, 1850s

QUARTER-PLATE DAGUERREOTYPE
84.XT.1581.19

THE J. PAUL GETTY MUSEUM, LOS ANGELES

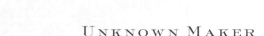

WHEN I SEE THIS PICTURE, I see Negroes barely visible at different levels in far-reaching spaces. And, though they must have prepared the private fires and helped to maintain this stage house for the accommodation of travelers, this inherent freedom to travel in America was not theirs. It makes me think that within this cordial setting, each discerned Negro was confined to this place. Though we do not know whether these Negroes were slave or free, in some ways, when the photographer went to take this outdoor view, he was taking a picture of a little world.

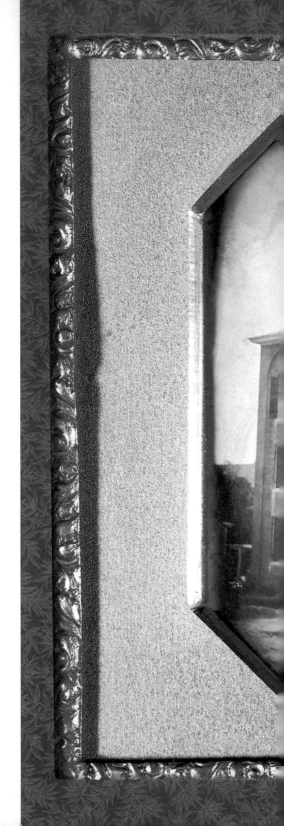

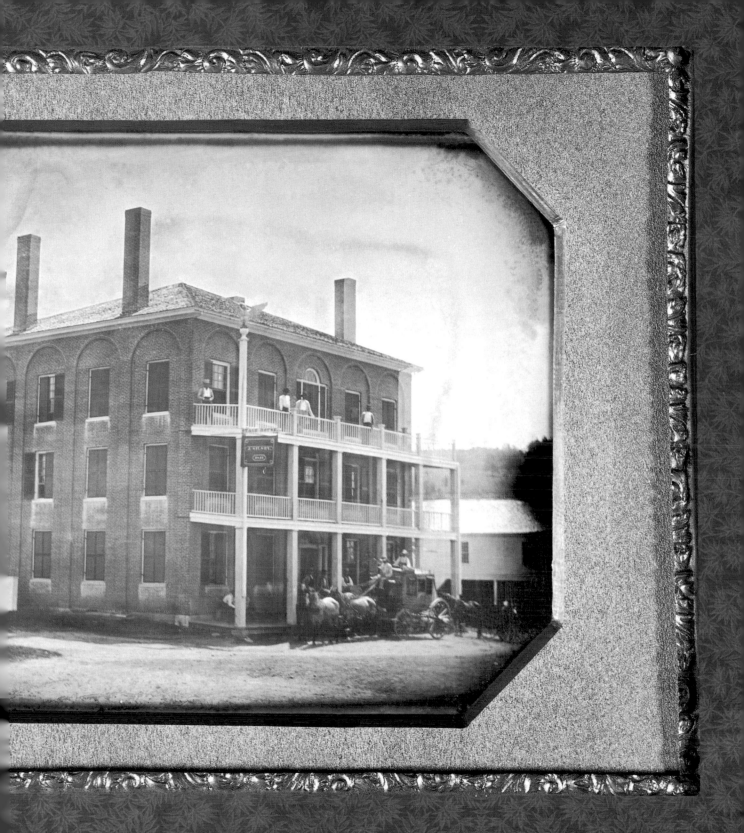

UNKNOWN MAKER
American School

Old Woman Wearing Bonnet, ca. 1850

SIXTH-PLATE DAGUERREOTYPE

JACKIE NAPOLEAN WILSON COLLECTION

THIS WOMAN WOULD HAVE BEEN BORN BEFORE the American Revolution. In all probability, she was born free and never lived to see the demise of American slavery. The three books on the table were purposely stacked there to show that she could read. Although it was unlawful throughout the country to teach slaves, there were free blacks who could read and write. The very small case on top of the books is the case in which this daguerreotype was placed. Early photography tended to exaggerate extremities such as her hands. This was probably the first time that she had her picture taken as shown by the prideful expression on her face.

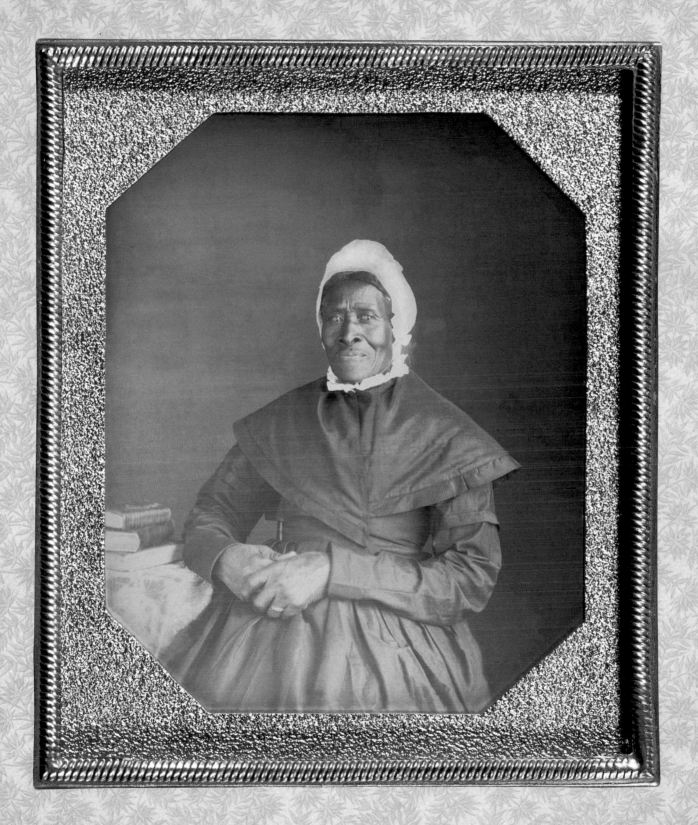

UNKNOWN MAKER

American School

Woman with Painted Backdrop, ca. 1850

SIXTH-PLATE DAGUERREOTYPE

JACKIE NAPOLEAN WILSON COLLECTION

THIS WOMAN WEARING A TIARA AND A scriber's chain in elegant appointment has the Monument Square depicting Baltimore in the actual or painted background. She was of obvious means and class. Women of stature fancied tiaras such as Queen Victoria's. The makeup and carriage of this lady are highly suggestive of her being Elizabeth Keckley, the modiste (dressmaker) and personal maid to Mary Todd Lincoln in the Executive Mansion.

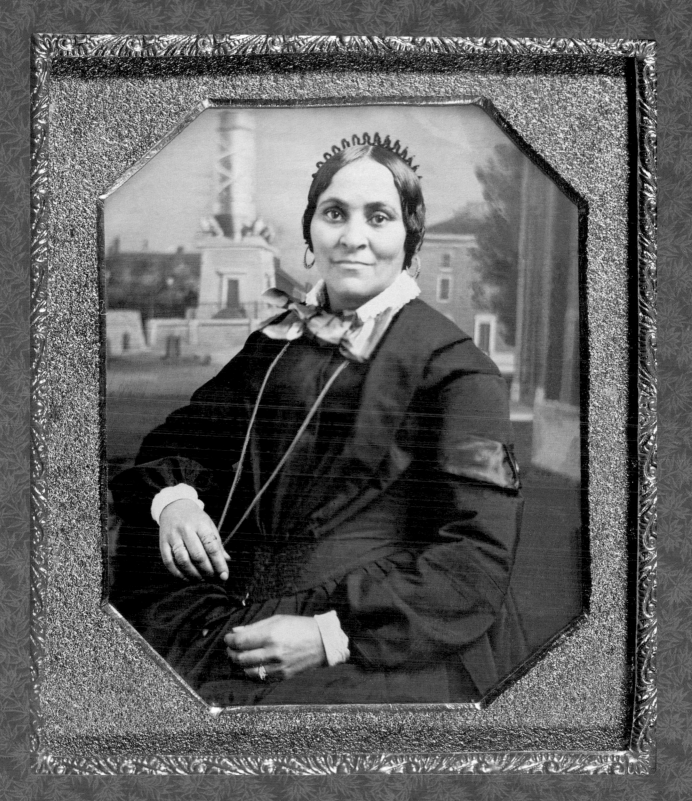

UNKNOWN MAKER

American School

Portrait of a New York Lady of Letters, ca. 1850

SIXTH-PLATE DAGUERREOTYPE

JACKIE NAPOLEAN WILSON COLLECTION

THIS PORTRAIT OF A WOMAN WITH HER HEAD poised on her hand, the open book in her other hand, appears to depict an intellectual. She is in the traditional pose of the "melancholic," a tradition that may well precede the Middle Ages back even into antiquity. Artists and thinkers and poets were traditionally thought to be melancholic, moody, depressed, lost in thought— precisely the pose of this woman. ❧ From her costume, hairstyle and jewelry, this woman would appear to be affluent. She may have come to the daguerreian parlor with several other people—probably her family—whose likenesses are represented in three daguerreotypes in cases on the table.

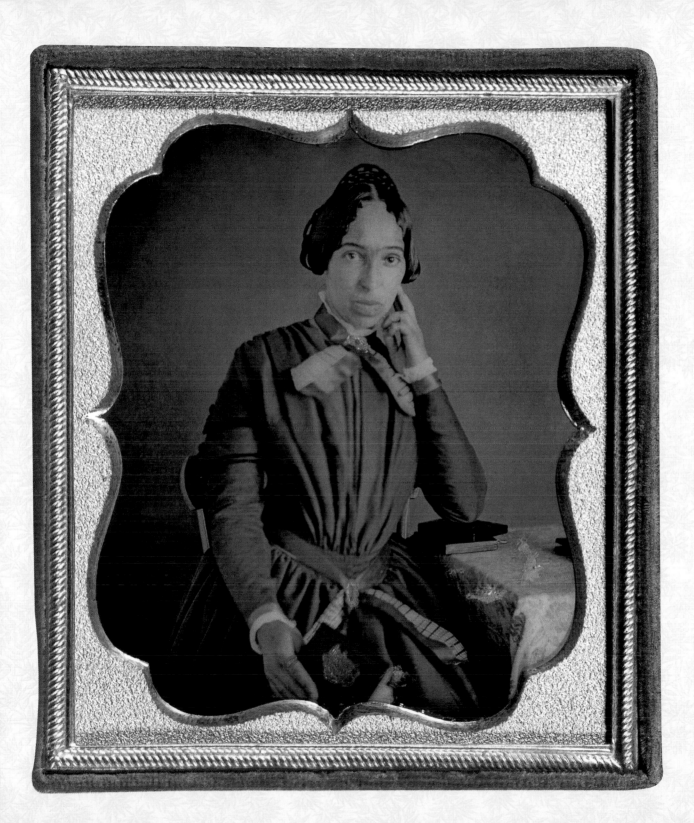

ALEXANDER S. THOMAS

American, active Cincinnati, 1850s–70s

Betty Easton, ca. 1855

SIXTH-PLATE DAGUERREOTYPE

THE LIKENESS OF BETTY EASTON WAS TAKEN by her son, Alexander S. Thomas. Thomas was a partner to the African-American photographer James P. Ball. Looking like a diva with coiffured hair and well-appointed shawl, there is a magnetism in her eyes and a sense of pride for her son, the photographer.

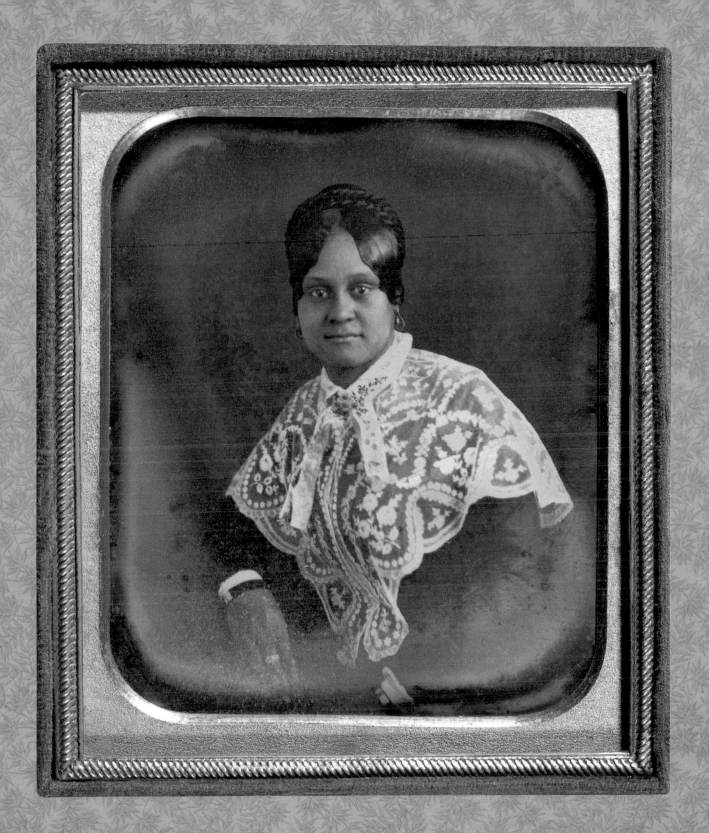

UNKNOWN MAKER

American School

Portrait of a Seated Black Woman, 1855–60

SIXTH-PLATE AMBROTYPE

84.XT.404.18

THE J. PAUL GETTY MUSEUM, LOS ANGELES

B Y PLACING HER HAND ON HER ABDOMEN, this woman may be signaling that she is with child. Pregnant women are seldom shown in early photographs, perhaps owing to Victorian mores. This woman wears rarely seen African trade beads, a form of currency in Africa, which may well symbolize her awareness of her ancestral links.

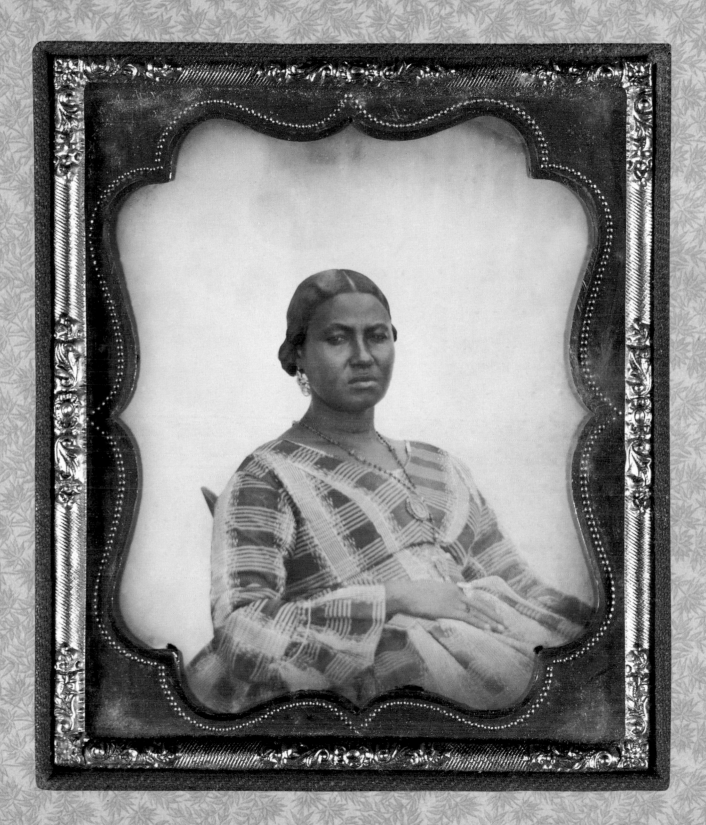

UNKNOWN MAKER

American School

Portrait of a Well-Dressed Young Boy, ca. 1857–58

SIXTH-PLATE AMBROTYPE

84.XT.1568.36

THE J. PAUL GETTY MUSEUM, LOS ANGELES

THIS IS NOT THE AVERAGE NEGRO CHILD OF the slave era. The parents of this child were the exception in society and no doubt pursued one of the lucrative occupations or trades open to African-Americans, such as barber, dressmaker, carpenter, or the clergy. ❧ One can wonder at what age children of color learned that they were deemed inferior in American society. At what age did white children perceive their Negro counterparts with contempt to the point of intolerance? What would he feel, as a free Negro, when he heard comments about his heritage and realized that he, despite his present status, was yet viewed as subhuman and the potential property of some slave hunter?

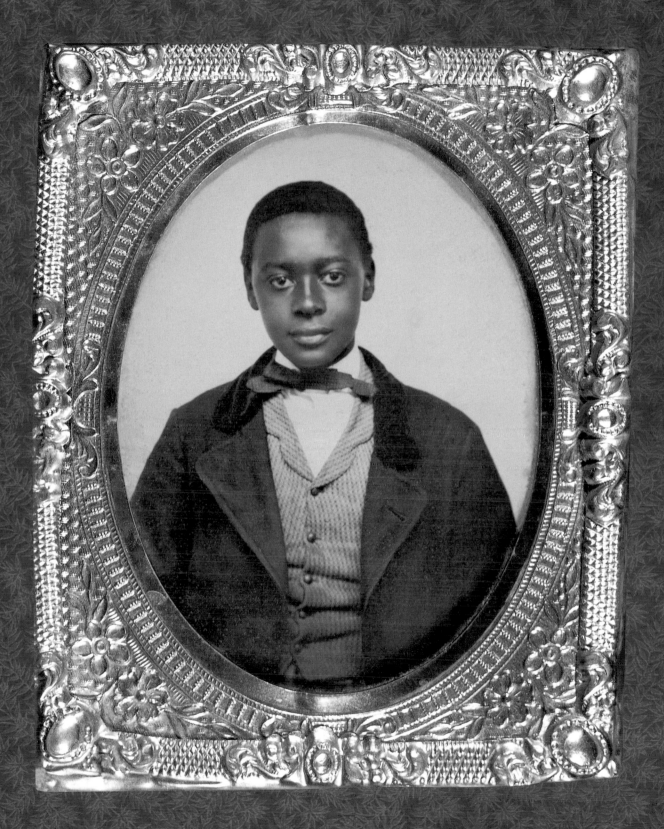

UNKNOWN MAKER

American School

Portrait of a Young Boy in Fine Clothes, ca. 1850s

NINTH-PLATE DAGUERREOTYPE
84.XT.1582.18

THE J. PAUL GETTY MUSEUM, LOS ANGELES

THIS YOUNG BOY APPEARS TO HAVE BEEN born to a wealthy and influential family, and per-haps had private instructors, an imitation of white society. If not for his race, one might suppose that he was a student of an elite academy. The photographer captured a poise of genteel control. This boy appears sheltered from the realities of existence in his time.

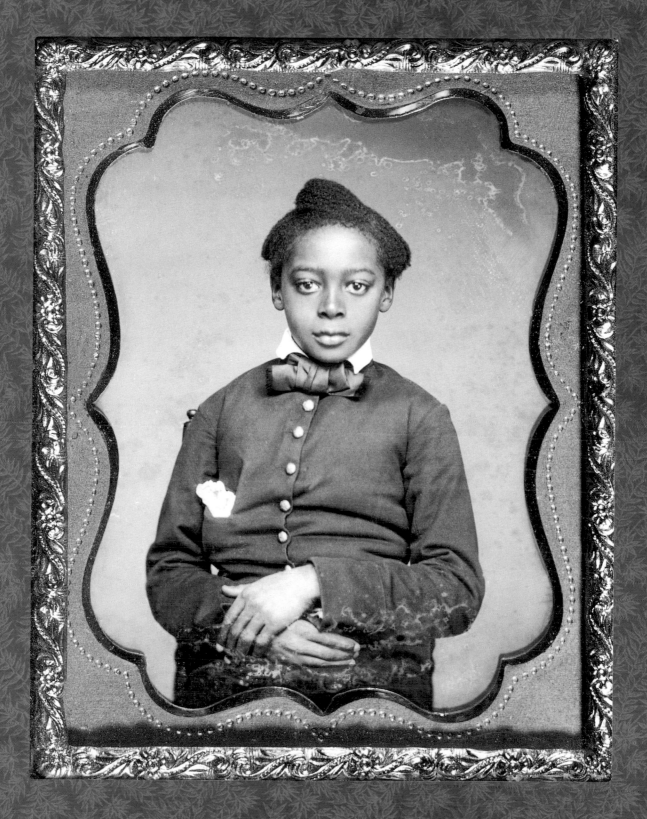

UNKNOWN MAKER

American School

Boy Seated in Spindle Chair, ca. 1860

SIXTH-PLATE AMBROTYPE

JACKIE NAPOLEAN WILSON COLLECTION

THERE WERE AFRICAN-AMERICAN CHILDREN who were from affluent homes in both North and South, but it was quite unusual. Perhaps this child's parents owned a business; his father could have been a barber; his mother may have been a dressmaker. Not many black children wore such elaborately layered clothing. It is the innocence, pride, and dignity seen in this boy's face that impresses us today.

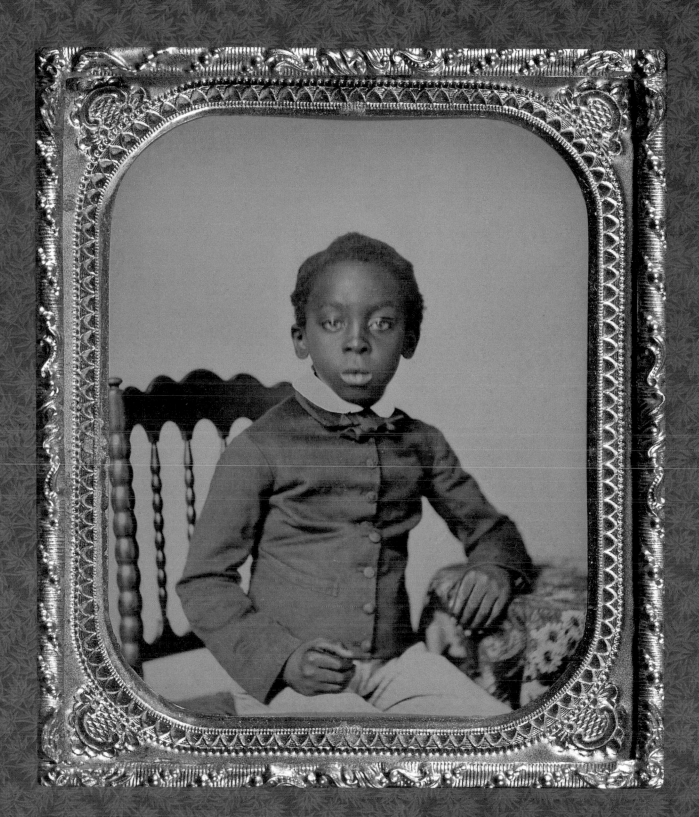

UNKNOWN MAKER

American School

Postmortem Portrait of a Child, ca. 1855–57

SIXTH-PLATE DAGUERREOTYPE

84.XT.1582.7

THE J. PAUL GETTY MUSEUM, LOS ANGELES

THIS BLACK DRAPING, IN ITSELF A MEMORIAL, tells us that this is a postmortem daguerreotype. While this type of photograph was common in white society of the 1840s and 1850s, this is a rare image of the dead child of free African-Americans. Some slave parents thought it nearly best for their children not to survive and to face the perils of slavery. This child was wanted, needed, and had a place among the free. ❧ Infants and children died of early childhood diseases more often in the nineteenth century than today. For those who could afford it, a picture of a deceased relative was cherished, a symbol of the love and devotion parents felt for their children even in death.

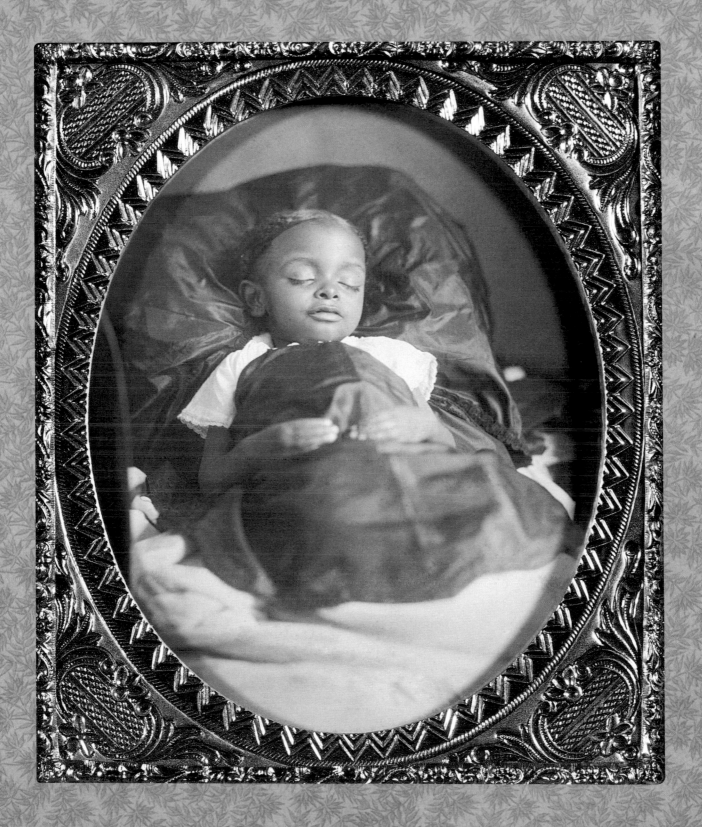

UNKNOWN MAKER

American School

Portrait of a Young Man, ca. 1855

SIXTH-PLATE DAGUERREOTYPE

84.XT.442.10

THE J. PAUL GETTY MUSEUM, LOS ANGELES

THE DIMENSIONS IN THIS DAGUERREOTYPE suggest that abolitionists orchestrated this image. This young mulatto man, dressed in oversize clothing, is seen from head to toe, although full-figured daguerreotypes are less often seen in early studio photography than sitting and waist-up portraits. Written letters of disdain are recorded in antebellum history, sent to former owners by persons who stole their freedom. This man is his own courier and the "letter" in his left hand—a skunk—is his message. He sends his "letter" with an air of confidence. So it seems that someone assisted this young man to "face" his oppressor. The photograph delivers the scorn.

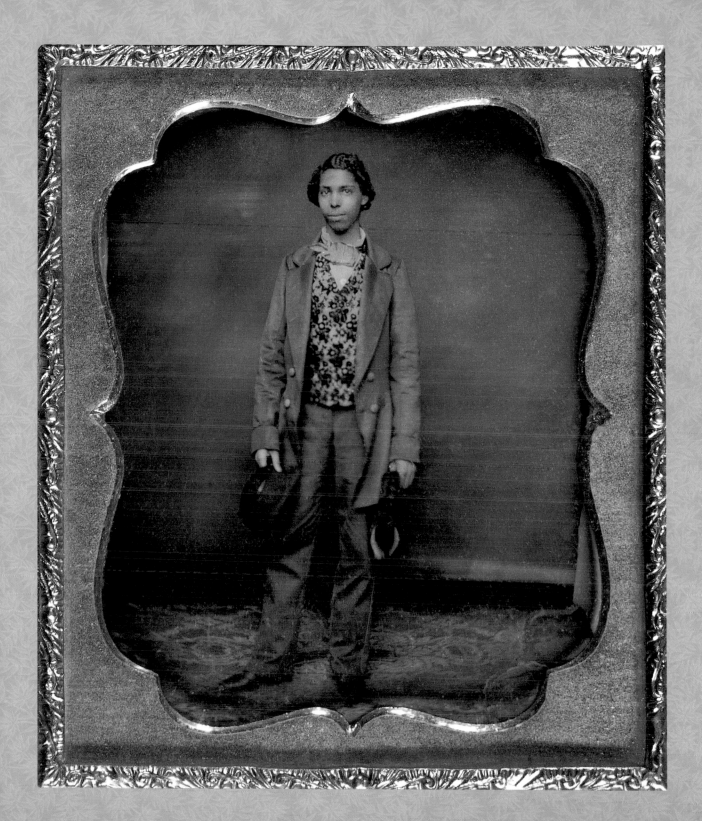

UNKNOWN MAKER

American School

Portrait of a Black Man Wearing a Bow Tie, ca. 1856

SIXTH-PLATE DAGUERREOTYPE

84.XT.441.3

THE J. PAUL GETTY MUSEUM, LOS ANGELES

THE MAN DEPICTED IN THIS DAGUERREOTYPE seems to be saying, "I have arrived," and anticipating the reply of someone waiting for him. This well-dressed man, endowed with pure African features, is typical of men who sometimes fared better as ex-slaves than many free-born blacks and mulattos in the North. The experience of slavery inspired many people to purchase land and hold fast to family values after they were freed. Daguerreotypes were often presented by a suitor to the family of the woman he was courting, so the portrait could be circulated to other family members for recognition and approval. This practice became commonplace a decade later in the era of the cartes-de-visite.

Still, there was slavery in freedom. In certain parts of the country, a black man had to carry freedom papers. Job opportunities were limited and steeped with prejudices, even from the newly arrived immigrants. Often, the only available employment was that of waiter, porter, cook, bootblack, groom, and laborer— all low in status.

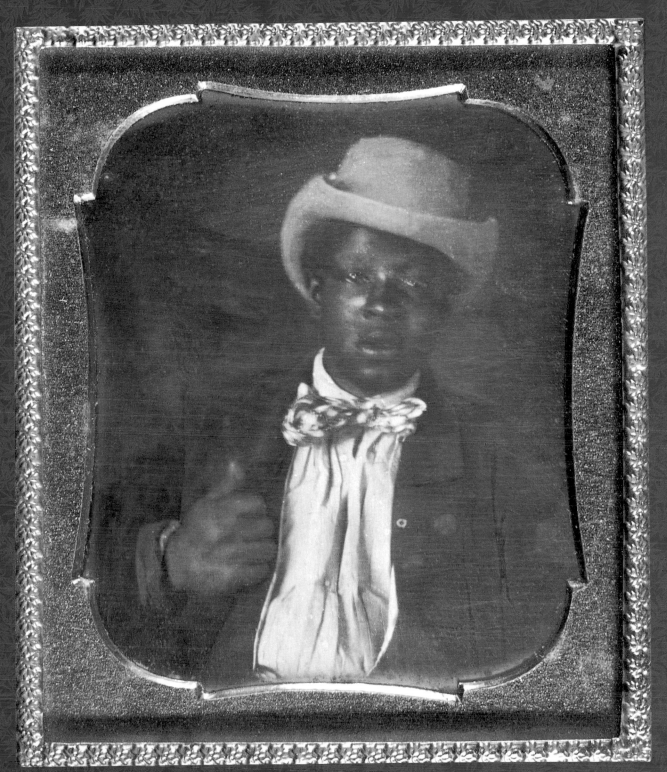

UNKNOWN MAKER

American School

Venerable Elder, ca. 1860

NINTH-PLATE AMBROTYPE

JACKIE NAPOLEAN WILSON COLLECTION

THIS DISTINGUISHED MAN, SEVENTY OR eighty years of age, wears clothes dating from decades before this ambrotype was made. He projects the aura of a man who was born free, so he may have lived in the Northern states where slavery had been abolished before the Revolutionary War. Some slaves from the North were sold to the South, some were freed by their owners, and some African-Americans had always been free in America even well before the Republic's inception.

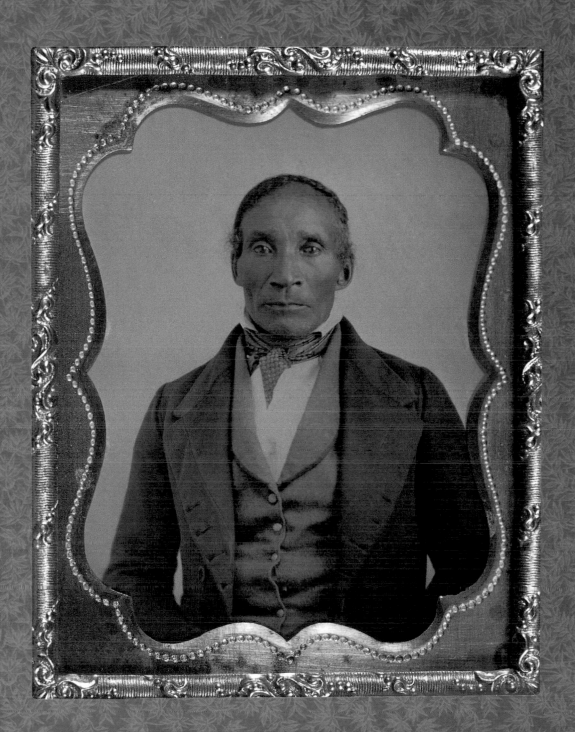

UNKNOWN MAKER

American School

Stoic Man, ca. 1860

NINTH-PLATE AMBROTYPE

JACKIE NAPOLEAN WILSON COLLECTION

THIS STOIC FACE SUGGESTS WISDOM, BUT HIS visage does not appear to fit with his formal attire, as he must have led a hard, industrious existence. Photographers did not often ask more than one pose of a subject because the process was so involved. But with this off-centered position, the subject is more revealed because the wide unbalanced open space rises to his piercing eyes.

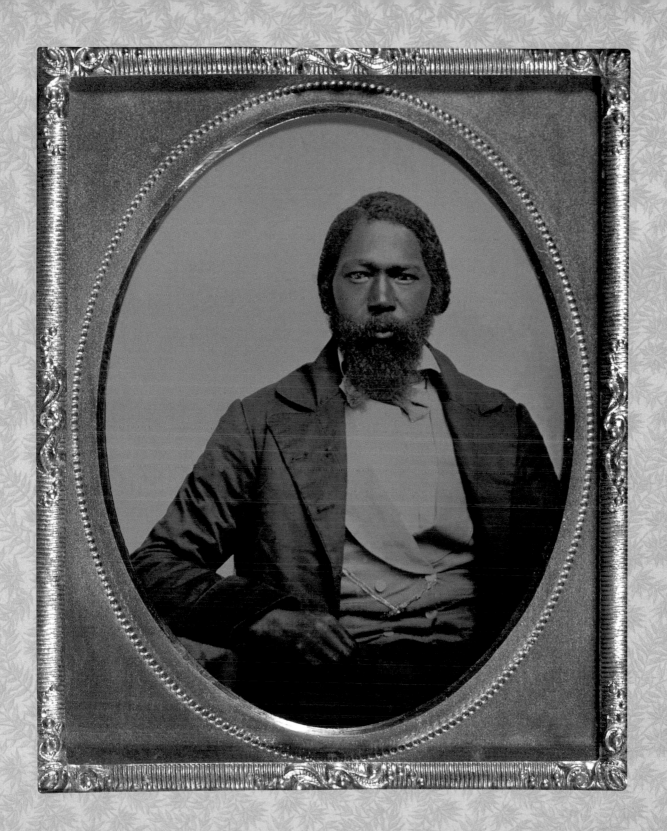

UNKNOWN MAKER

American School

A Philadelphia Man with Plaid Cravat, ca. 1860

SIXTH-PLATE AMBROTYPE

JACKIE NAPOLEAN WILSON COLLECTION

W E KNOW THAT THIS MAN IS FROM Philadelphia from an inscription on the back of the ambrotype. He is meticulously dressed, which shows that he lived in the highest echelon of the African-American community in his city. How far away from home could this man have traveled? What was the manner of his speech? Where are his descendants today? This image is nearly a deception, because hardly any African-Americans in his time were living beyond abject poverty, both in the "City of Brotherly Love" and through-out the country.

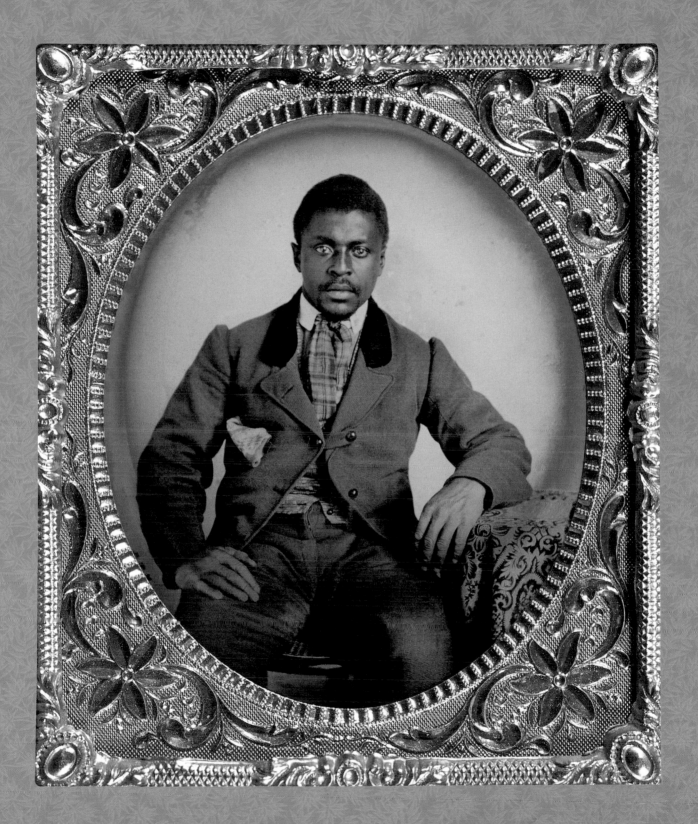

UNKNOWN MAKER

American School

Mulatto Man, ca. 1850

SIXTH-PLATE DAGUERREOTYPE

JACKIE NAPOLEAN WILSON COLLECTION

PART WHITE AND PART BLACK, THIS MAN is halfway between two races. In North and South, there were free Negro communities that numbered more mulattoes than those of pure African heritage. This nearly white appearance in some African-Americans caused many Caucasians to develop an aversion toward slavery. In the South, mulattoes with even more distinctly white features were slaves; some were sold by their white fathers and relatives who knew of their blood relationships. This man may have had a mulatto mother and may have been sent to the North by his white father to be free, relocated, and educated. Some mulattoes were able to escape into the white race, with their African genealogy buried forever.

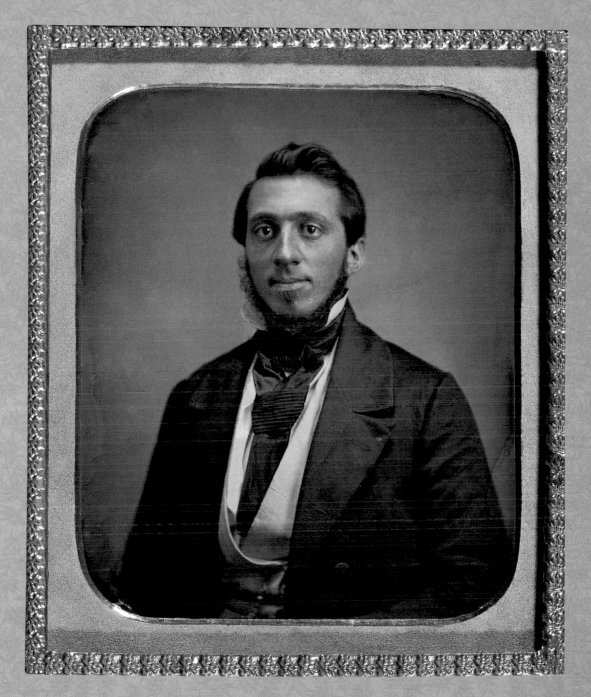

UNKNOWN MAKER

American School

Portrait of a Mulatto Man, ca. 1857

SIXTH-PLATE DAGUERREOTYPE
84.XT.404.12

THE J. PAUL GETTY MUSEUM, LOS ANGELES

D O NOT BE DECEIVED WHEN YOU SEE A well-dressed Negro man in historical photography. Most Negro men lived in abject poverty. The stature and respect bestowed upon this man was limited to his immediate environment, composed mainly of blacks who could barely afford such fine clothing. When he left his community he had to be as humble as a slave. The free Negro male had many social barriers to overcome. No matter how expensive or tasteful his appearance, he never rose above the servant role; he was forbidden by custom to look whites in the eye.

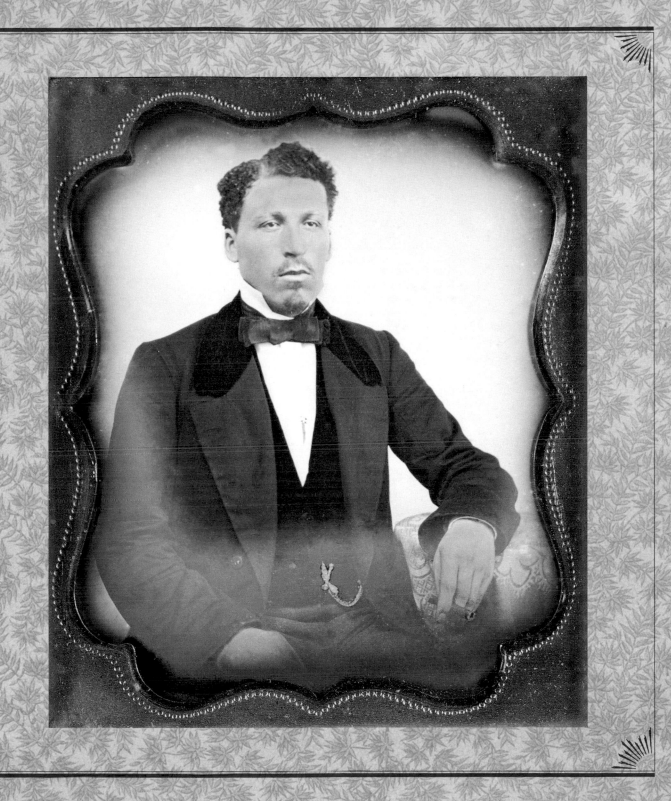

UNKNOWN MAKER

American School

Man in White Vest, ca. 1860

SIXTH-PLATE AMBROTYPE

JACKIE NAPOLEAN WILSON COLLECTION

THERE IS A NATURAL RELAXATION IN THE appearance of this man that suggests he was used to this composure. His delicate fingers and groomed hairstyle indicate that he may have been a barber, an allowable occupation for free Negroes at that time. He would have been relaxed and in contact with his peers in a commercial setting. Typically, by law and custom Negroes could not gather beyond certain numbers, but a barber establishment would have been a place of contact where permissible events of community interest were posted, as was allowed practice at that time.

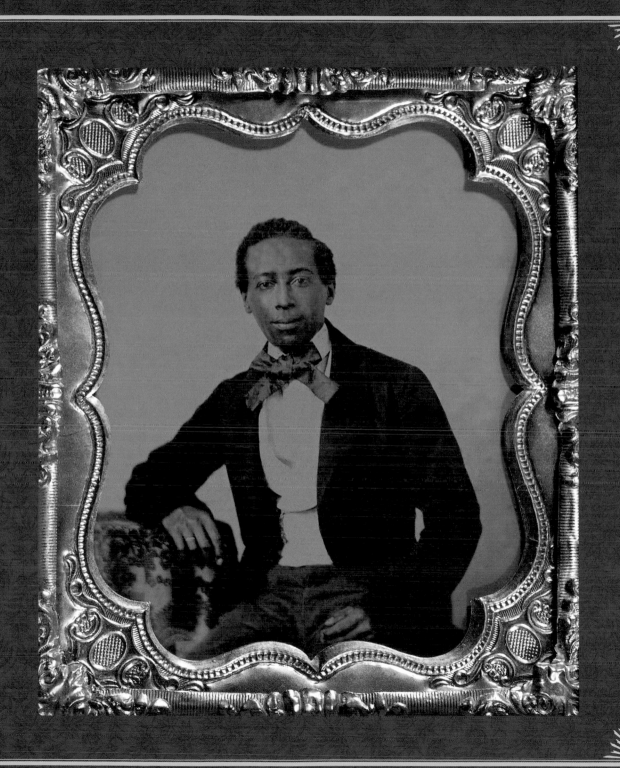

UNKNOWN MAKER

American School

Man with Hands on His Knees, ca. 1865

SIXTH-PLATE TINTYPE

JACKIE NAPOLEAN WILSON COLLECTION

CURIOSITY AND COOPERATION ABOUND in this man's expression. The pleasantry and mildness of personality captured by this image show on his face; his slightly turned head and his curious eyes suggest humanity.

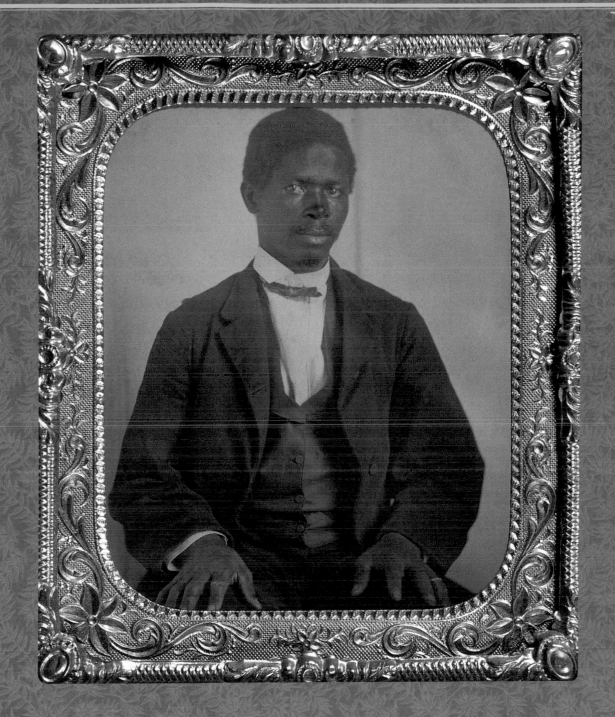

UNKNOWN MAKER
American School

Man with Amiable Smile, ca. 1860

SIXTH-PLATE TINTYPE

JACKIE NAPOLEAN WILSON COLLECTION

BECAUSE OF THE STILLNESS NEEDED FOR the process of early photography, the naturalness of a pleasant face is often not revealed. Here it comes through exuberantly, and it makes one wonder whether it was the sheer naturalness of the sitter or a pleasant rapport between the photographer and sitter that defied the norm. When you see such a person, be mindful that these well-dressed men were subjected to the black codes and ordinances of curfew, the laws regarding group gathering, and a general societal contempt which believed all African-Americans to be inferior.

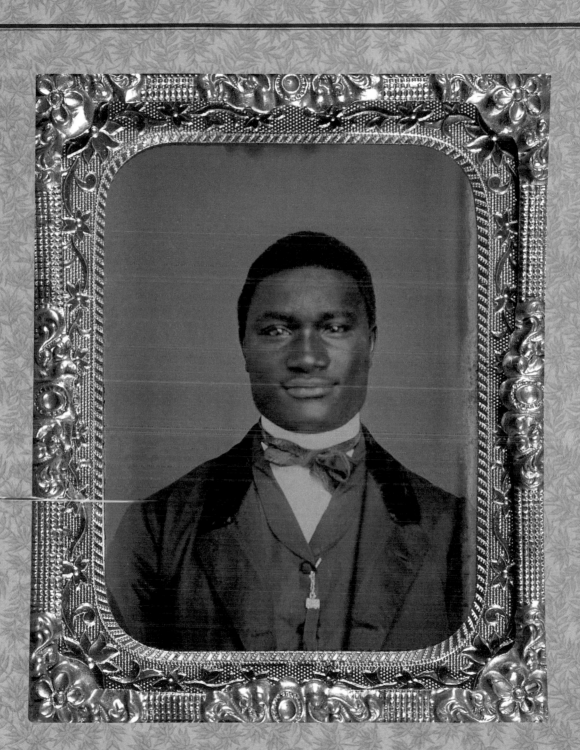

UNKNOWN MAKER
American School

Reflective Man, Cincinnati, Ohio, ca. 1855

SIXTH-PLATE DAGUERREOTYPE

JACKIE NAPOLEAN WILSON COLLECTION

THIS MAN IS REFLECTING, BUT WE HAVE NO window into his mind. To see his face turned inward suggests he had pleasant things to reminisce about, but while the camera captured the essence, we will never know the thought.

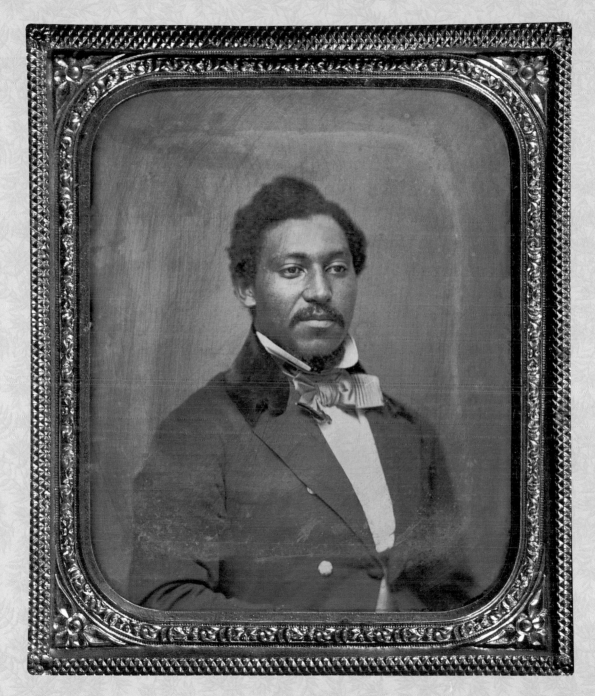

UNKNOWN MAKER

American School

Man with Square Goatee, ca. 1860

SIXTH-PLATE AMBROTYPE

JACKIE NAPOLEAN WILSON COLLECTION

THIS MAN'S FACIAL WHISKERS RESEMBLE the pharaonic beards of ancient Egypt. In his time he would have been referred to as a "Negro," but today, numerous terms are used to describe people out of Africa. Nevertheless, it is historically accurate to call an African-American a Negro at that time.

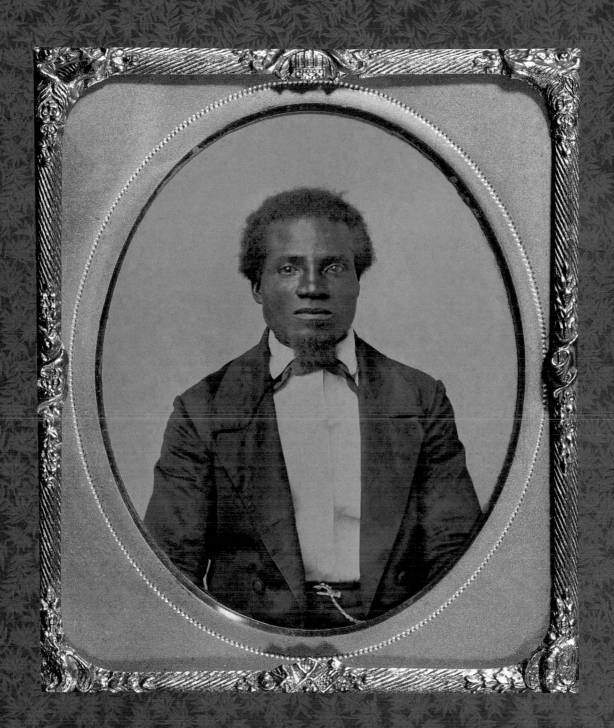

UNKNOWN MAKER

American School

Fireman in Uniform Holding a Brass Musical Instrument, ca. 1850

SIXTH-PLATE DAGUERREOTYPE

84.XT.1582.3

THE J. PAUL GETTY MUSEUM, LOS ANGELES

NO ONE WAS WARY OF THIS MAN. HE HOLDS his bugle and wears a medal depicting the rescue of a fire victim. History is full of accounts of fire devastation. Philadelphia had a notable fire on July 9, 1850. This city had black bandsmen who would perform in formal Firemen's Parades. Whites performed in concert bands, but not typically in marching bands until the 1850s.

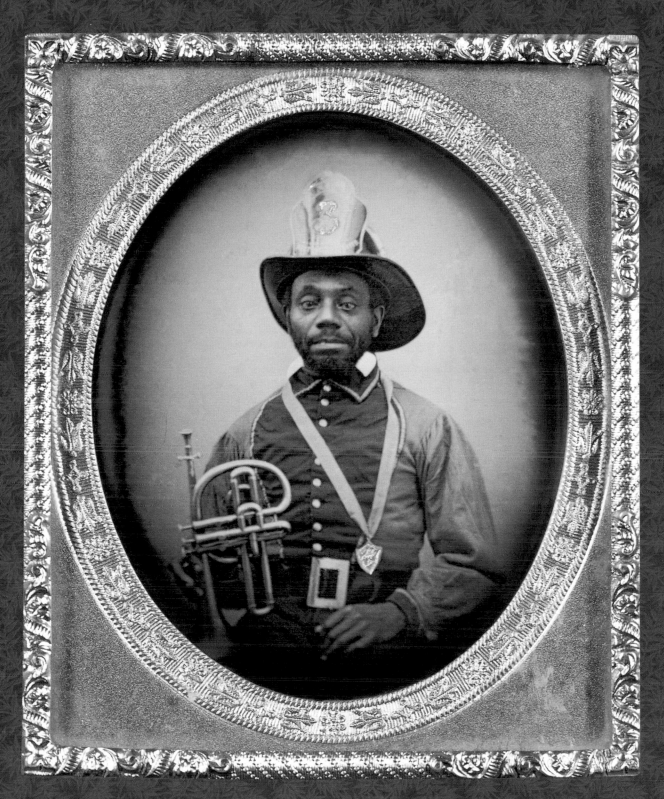

UNKNOWN MAKER

American School

Slave with Pedigreed Heifer and Bull, ca. 1856

TWO SIXTH-PLATE DAGUERREOTYPES
84.XT.1582.15.1–2

THE J. PAUL GETTY MUSEUM, LOS ANGELES

THIS PAIR OF DAGUERREOTYPES MOUNTED in a single-hinged case is a record of a pedigree in livestock. Ironically, the slave was not accorded the

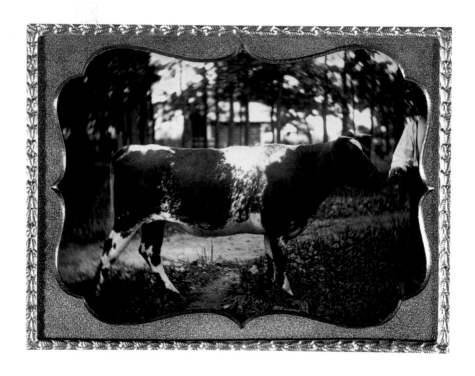

same value in terms of his own lineage. The slave's function was as a handler, trained to emphasize and market the best features of the animal.

Portraits of animals were uncommon. However, with the position of the nearly hidden slave, the photograph becomes more a showing of the owner's social and political stance on slavery rather than the intended commission of preserving a prize heifer and bull for posterity.

The handler was probably himself once displayed like an animal at auction and purchased and used for breeding. Did this slave know his blood relatives? He may not even have known who his parents were. Did his children know who he was? Could he form a family of his own?

Though the photographer did his commissioned work to illustrate the cattle, he left a deeper, more meaningful record for posterity.

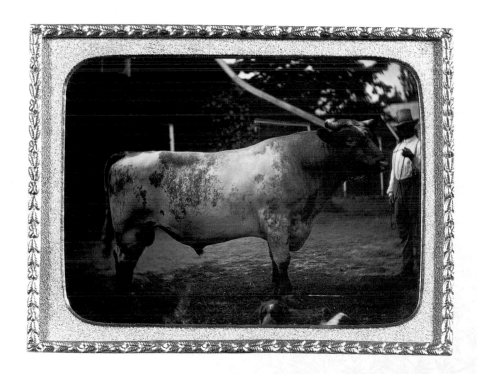

UNKNOWN MAKER

American School

Blacksmith, ca. 1860

SIXTH-PLATE TINTYPE

JACKIE NAPOLEAN WILSON COLLECTION

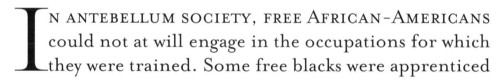

IN ANTEBELLUM SOCIETY, FREE AFRICAN-AMERICANS could not at will engage in the occupations for which they were trained. Some free blacks were apprenticed and practiced a trade before they were manumitted, or liberated, from the owner, or bought their own freedom. White Americans and immigrants viewed free black artisans as competition in the workplace and refused to labor alongside them. This contributed to poverty and suffering for many free blacks, who could only get menial jobs. This man was able to practice his trade, and the photograph is testimony to the pride he took in this accomplishment. Could this be a portrait of James Pennington, the fugitive blacksmith, whose printed account of how he gained freedom brought him celebrity in 1849?

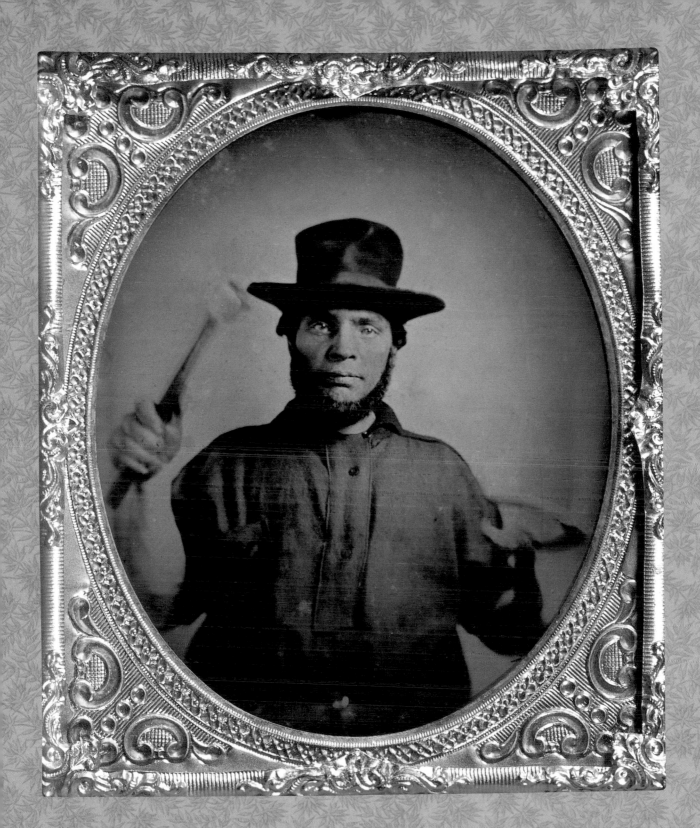

UNKNOWN MAKER

American School

Man in Paisley Vest, ca. 1848

SIXTH-PLATE DAGUERREOTYPE

JACKIE NAPOLEAN WILSON COLLECTION

MANY EARLY PHOTOGRAPHERS HAD BEEN portrait painters before the invention of photography. This craft carried over to the art of photography. The flower pot adds a touch of elegance to this image of a mulatto man, who may have been a person of high status in the community. He had adorned himself with a bold vest and a chain with a small medallion around his neck. A three-colored ribbon, perhaps red, white, and blue, is displayed proudly upon his shirt.

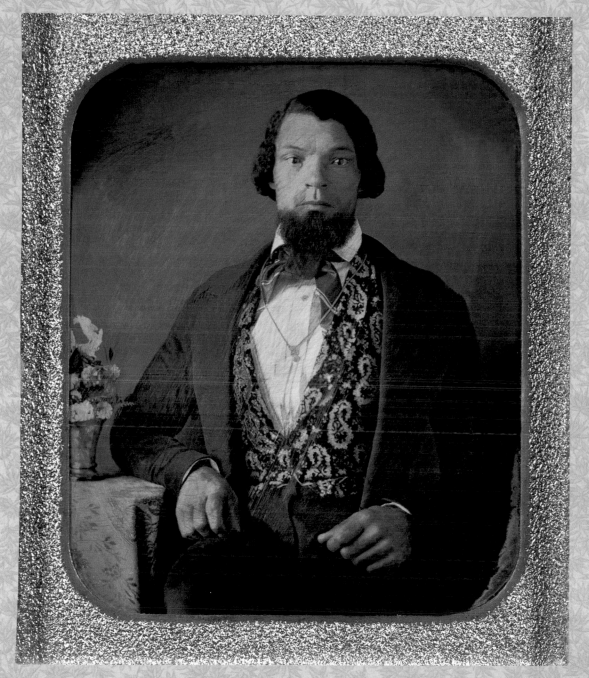

UNKNOWN MAKER

American School

Minister Wearing Spectacles, ca. 1855

SIXTH-PLATE DAGUERREOTYPE

JACKIE NAPOLEAN WILSON COLLECTION

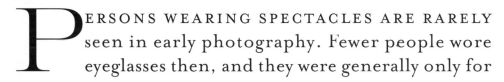

PERSONS WEARING SPECTACLES ARE RARELY seen in early photography. Fewer people wore eyeglasses then, and they were generally only for

reading and would have been removed for a portrait. Spectacles indicated not only that one needed and could afford eyeglasses but also that one could read and write, which in turn was evidence of an education. Of the African-Americans in the North who attained professional status, one out of ten was likely a minister or preacher.

African-American ministers typically addressed congregations of the same race. Where blacks attended white churches,

church decorum fostered segregated seating areas. The first entirely African-American church was established in Philadelphia in 1787 by Richard Allen, a former slave. Negro ministers not only instilled religion, but also taught their congregations through the Bible, fostered mutual aid associations, and through their churches provided a refuge for the downtrodden and a political arena that was not available to free African-Americans in society.

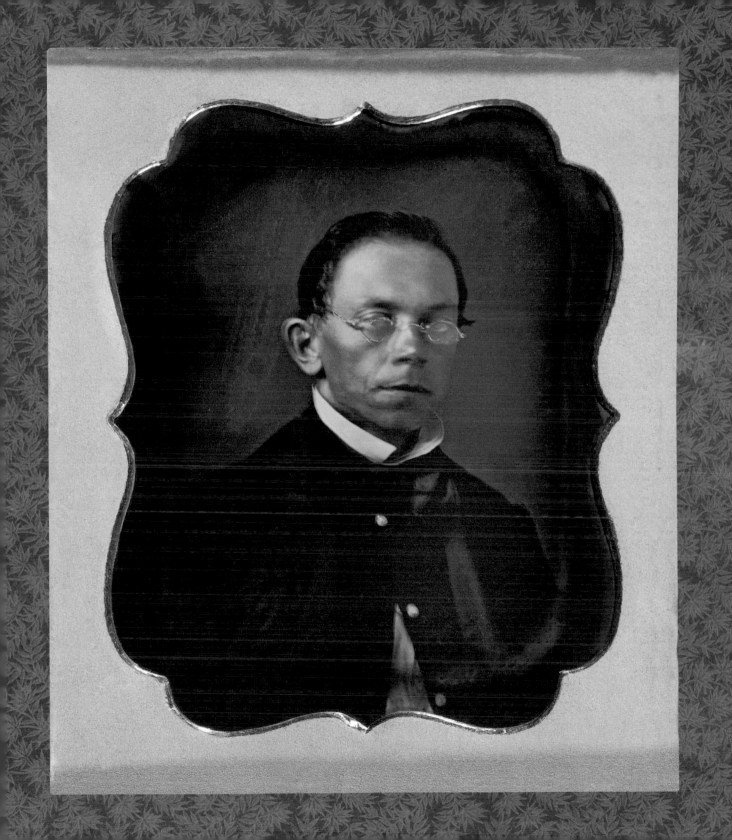

UNKNOWN MAKER

American School

The Smiling Man, 1860

SIXTH-PLATE DAGUERREOTYPE

84.XT.439.3

THE J. PAUL GETTY MUSEUM, LOS ANGELES

THIS MAN APPEARS TO BE A VICTORIOUS, clench-fisted professional boxer. He wears a sweat-shirt underneath, a boxer's apparel for his time,

and a sweat cloth drapes around his neck. His cheek has a swollen rise, his bottom lip is swollen and overall his face appears lumpy from the contest. Prizefighters fought mostly with their bare fists before 1886 and used brute strength since the aim was to knock out an opponent. This man's hands are positioned to show his art of hitting without being hit. His reward may have been prize money, which would make him a professional who could pay for his likeness. Slaveholders prepared slaves for this sport, but this is a free man taking personal glee in his victory.

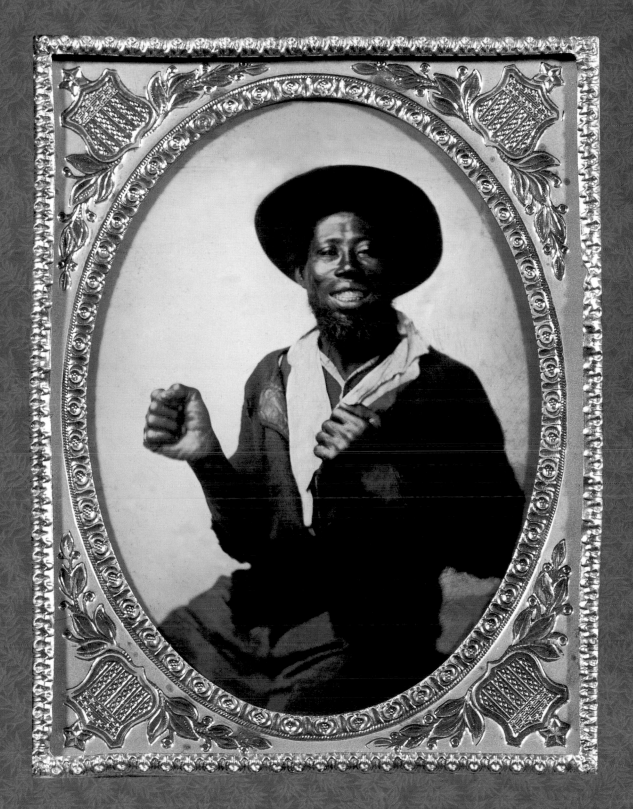

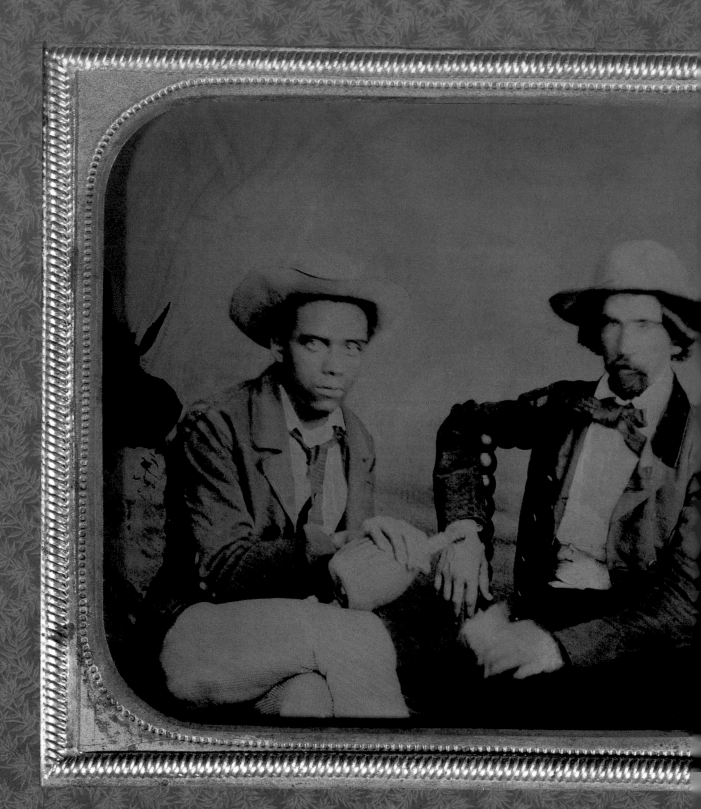

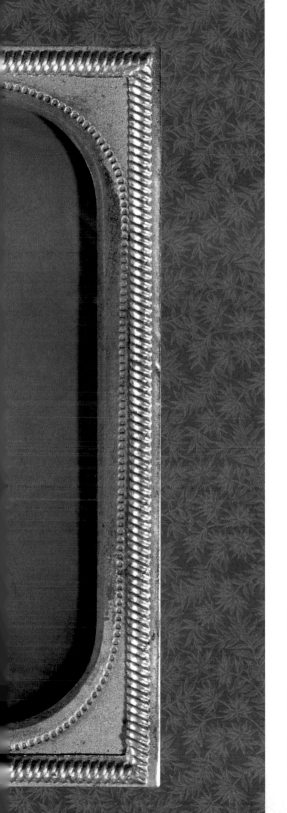

UNKNOWN MAKER

American School

Master and Servant, ca. 1860

SIXTH-PLATE AMBROTYPE

JACKIE NAPOLEAN WILSON COLLECTION

THESE TWO MEN ARE OF two distinct social orders even though they are shown seated side by side, as though they were equals. To make clear their roles, the Negro man is poised serving the master. Their clothing shows that the Negro man's costume is torn and tattered while the white man's is relatively new. The white man's hairstyle seems that of an actor but he could have easily been a gambler on a riverboat, a ruffian, or planter, a farmer or city dweller who owned a slave.

UNKNOWN MAKER

American School

Man and Slave Boy, ca. 1860

QUARTER-PLATE TINTYPE

JACKIE NAPOLEAN WILSON COLLECTION

THE MAN IN THIS TINTYPE IS NOT OF THE planter's class but appears to be a "would-be planter." There were whites in the South who aspired to own a slave since to do so was a symbol of wealth and a sign of rising fortune. One third of all Southerners owned no slaves and no land; one third owned land and no slaves; and one third owned both land and slaves. Ruggedly dressed slaves with bare feet are rarely seen in studio settings. This man flaunts his recent good fortune, evidenced by a new outfit for himself, a new gun, and new game bag, the fresh kill worn by the slave boy. Whether he owned or hired this slave, the boy, whose clothes have been supplied by his owner, shows no pride of possession, and we can only guess about his physical well-being.

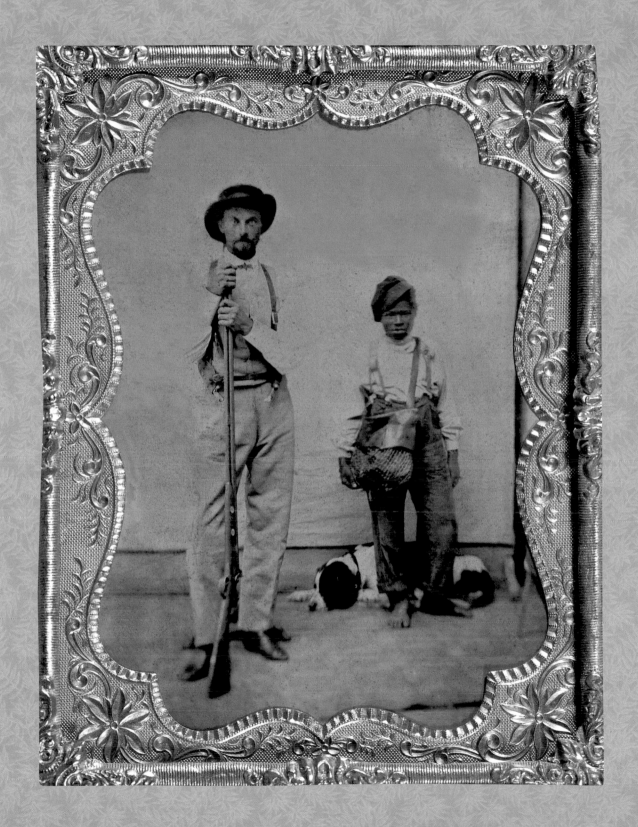

UNKNOWN MAKER

American School

Slave Nurse and Child, ca. 1850

SIXTH-PLATE DAGUERREOTYPE

JACKIE NAPOLEAN WILSON COLLECTION

THIS SLAVE GIRL'S FUNCTION WAS THAT OF A companion to the white child. Her position made her better off than most slave children. She seems to be well-fed and well-dressed, but her face is inscribed with inner pain. Slave children were often put to work in the field at an early age and would have one shirt and no shoes. Children of slaves were often cruelly separated from their families and sold at auctions, thus orphaned by the process of commerce. Although these children are positioned together, the slave girl was denied access to education and was forever destined to be a servant.

We can only imagine the pattern of behavior that existed between the two children. Was one dominant and the other submissive? Was theirs a relationship full of fun? Was mischief allowed by either one?

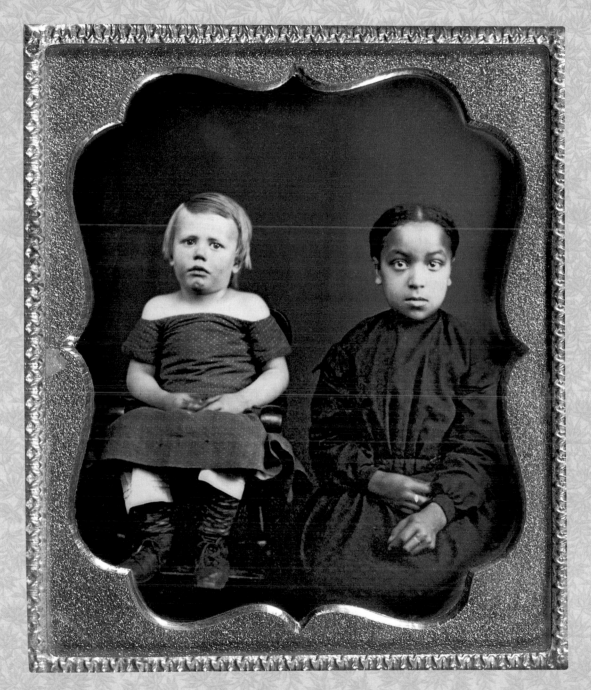

UNKNOWN MAKER

American School

Chamber Orchestra, January 16, 1865

QUARTER-PLATE TINTYPE

JACKIE NAPOLEAN WILSON COLLECTION

THIS QUARTER-PLATE TINTYPE HAS THREE dated stamps on it that reflect payment of a tax that helped finance the Union side of the Civil War.

We see here a five-string banjo, two violins, and a classical guitar. These were no doubt traveling musicians who would perform for segregated audiences in private homes, theaters, and health resorts. This authentic image contrasts with caricatures of African-Americans in Currier and Ives lithographs. Photographs of black people who achieved professional status in the arts are very rare, although at least one composer, Francis B. Johnson (1792–1844), was able to receive an acceptable reception in the antebellum society.

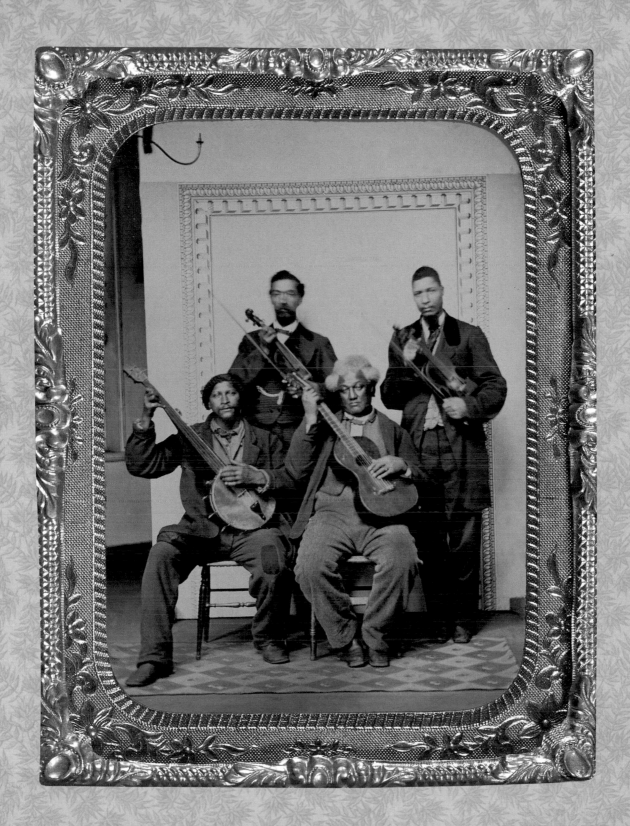

UNKNOWN MAKER

American School

Freemen of Color, ca. 1845–50

QUARTER-PLATE DAGUERREOTYPE

JACKIE NAPOLEAN WILSON COLLECTION

Arise, shine; for thy light is come, and the glory of the Lord is risen upon thee.

—ISAIAH 60:1

T

HIS IS THE EARLIEST KNOWN DAGUERREOTYPE of Frederick A. Douglass (right). It was taken perhaps a few years after he escaped from slavery in 1838,

maybe as young as twenty-three years of age in 1841. At times, given the state of the art, the image in a daguerreotype was reversed. So hold this picture to the mirror, and you will see how this man appeared in his early years in freedom before his rise to greatness.

The son of a Negro slave, Harriet Bailey, and an unknown white father (probably his mother's owner), Frederick took the surname Douglass from Sir Walter Scott's hero, Lord James of Douglass, in *The Lady of the Lake*. As an infant he was separated from his mother and sold to a Baltimore family, in which he was raised as a companion to the mistress's son, who taught him to read—which was against the law in all the slave states.

After his escape from bondage, he moved from Baltimore to New Bedford, Massachusetts, and began to speak out passionately against slavery. In August of 1841, he met the fervent and outspoken abolitionist leader William Lloyd Garrison, who witnessed his greatness at the annual meeting of the Massachusetts branch of the American Anti-Slavery Society. Garrison hired him as an agent for the Society and as its ambassador to the Nation. Douglass made speeches about liberty throughout Massachusetts and New York, and in other Northern states.

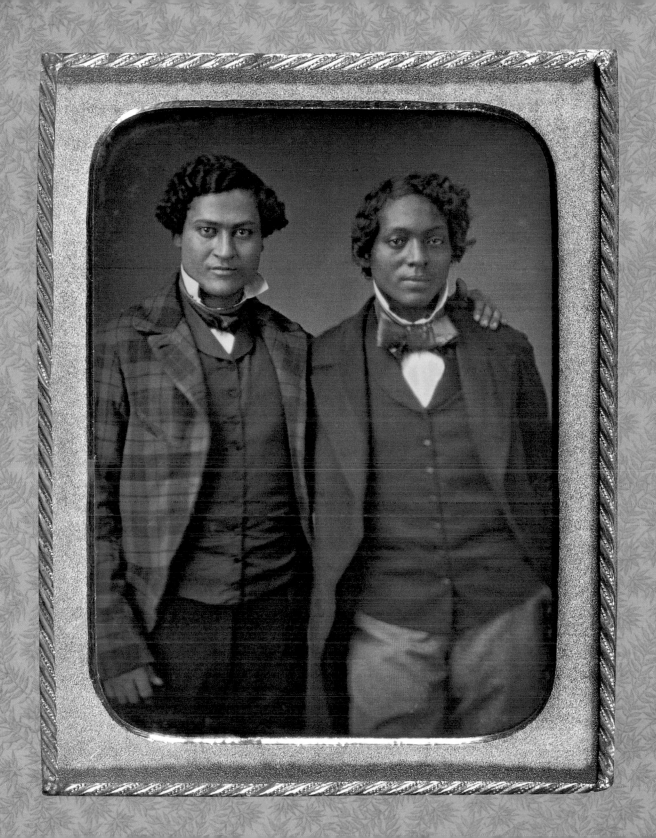

EZRA GREENLEAF WELD

American, 1801–1874

Frederick A. Douglass at Fugitive Slave Convention, Cazenovia, New York, August 22, 1850

SIXTH-PLATE DAGUERREOTYPE (REVERSED)

84.XT.1582.5

THE J. PAUL GETTY MUSEUM, LOS ANGELES

D ESPITE THE WHITE MAN'S AUTHORITY UNDER slavery, the antebellum South gave birth to a greatness in the form of Frederick Douglass, a fugitive slave who became the foremost African-American abolitionist. He is shown here in Cazenovia, New York, on August 22, 1850, addressing a meeting to protest the Fugitive Slave Law. This law stated that captured slave runaways could be forcibly returned to their Southern owners. The assembled crowd proved to be too large for the original meeting hall, and as no other building would accept them, they reconvened in a nearby apple orchard. Surrounded on the platform by the fiancée of a fugitive slave imprisoned in Washington and by two young girls who had sung for the crowd, Douglass said that his "banyan" was a small tree that "like the cause it sheltered has grown large and strong and imposing." Early images of political events are rare. Photographs of events that had worldwide implications are rarer still.

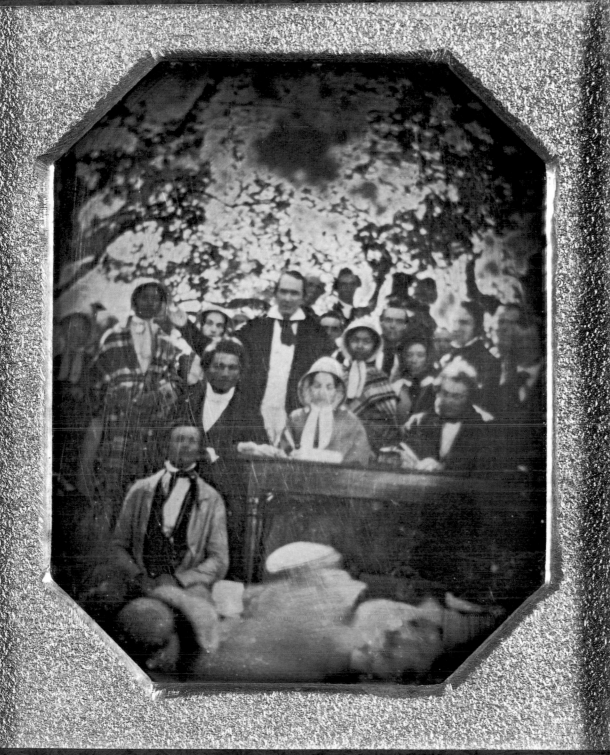

UNKNOWN MAKER

American School

Abolitionists at Niagara Falls, ca. 1860

WHOLE-PLATE AMBROTYPE

JACKIE NAPOLEAN WILSON COLLECTION

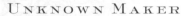

EVIDENCE SUGGESTS THIS scene may show two white men assisting a black man to freedom in Canada. Behind them is the the great natural spectacle of Niagara Falls, a fitting symbol for the abolitionist movement. They stand on the west bank of the Niagara River on Canadian soil. At this time there was no legal refuge in America for fugitive slaves. While Northern states did not allow slavery, neither did they quickly enact laws to help the cause. But there were many whites who aided fugitives because they believed that the laws of humanity and God were being violated by the slave system. They believed that the Republic could not stand unless people were free. The martyr John Brown stated his reason thus:

> *Upon the golden rule. I pity the poor in bondage that have none to help them; that is why I am here, not to gratify any personal animosity, revenge, or vindictive spirit. It is my sympathy with the oppressed and wronged, that are as good as you and as precious in the sight of God.*

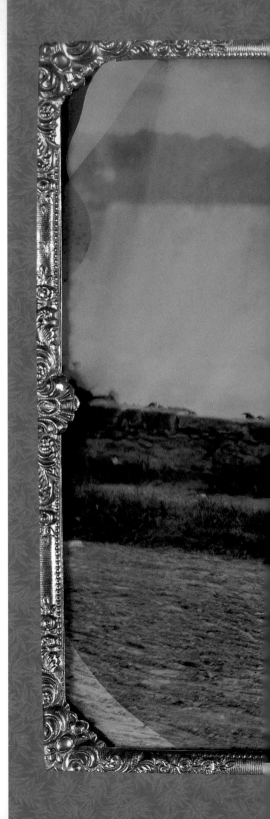

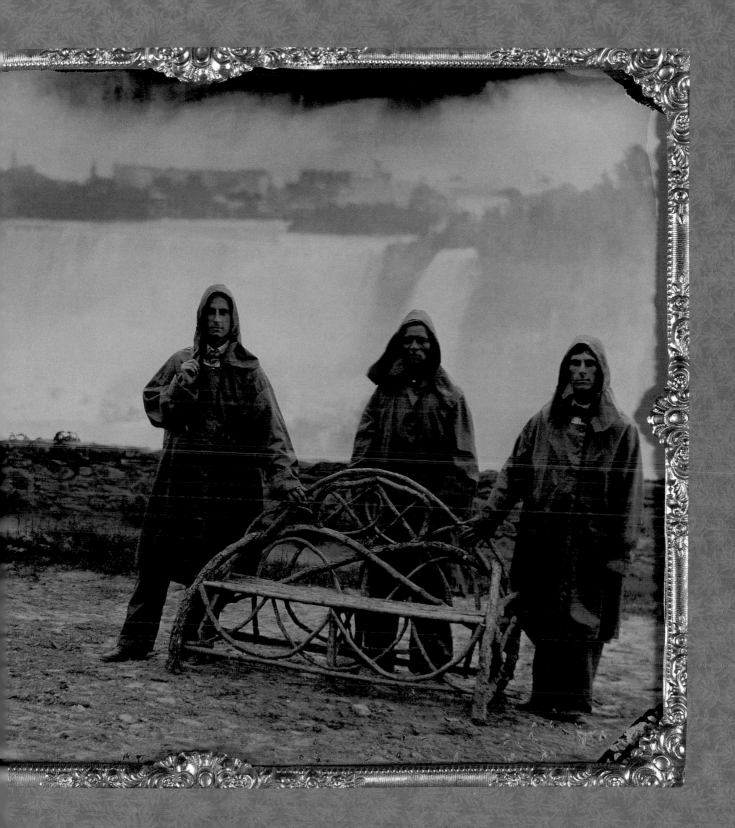

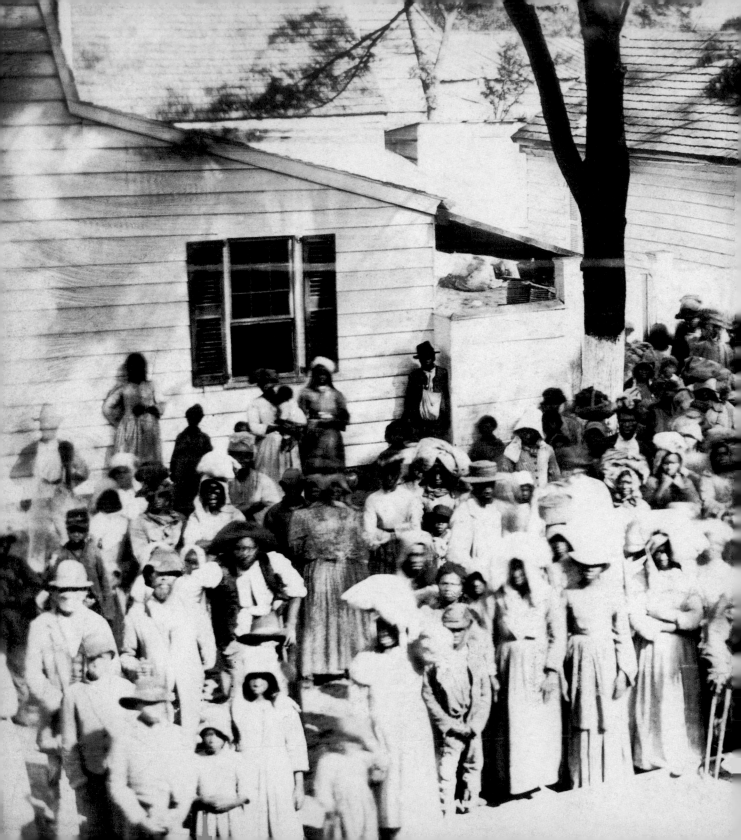

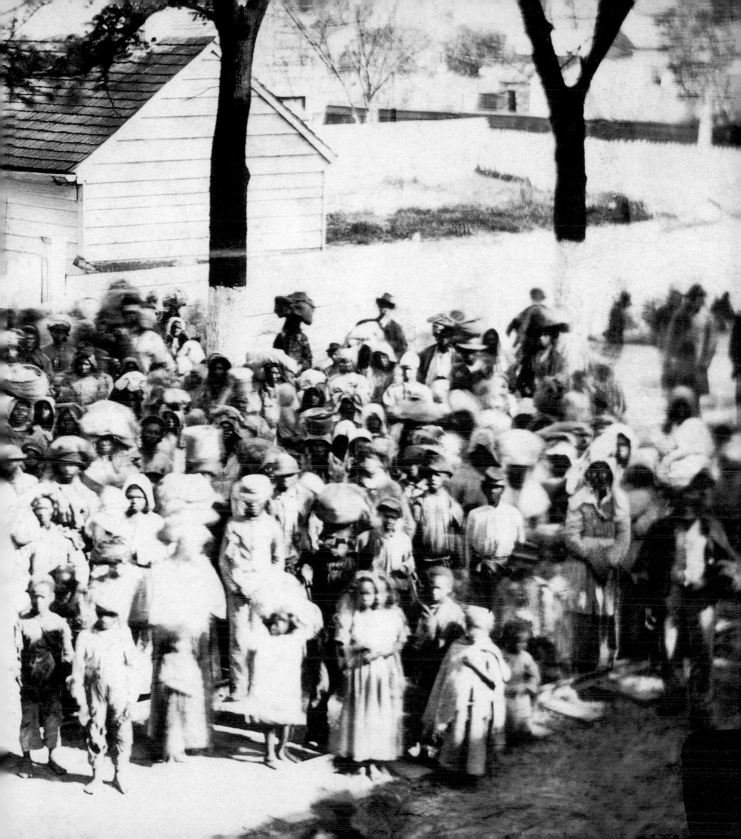

TIMOTHY H. O'SULLIVAN

American, ca. 1840–82

Slaves, Plantation of James Joyner Smith ("Old Fort Plantation"), Beaufort, South Carolina, 1862

ALBUMEN PRINT

84.XM.484.39

THE J. PAUL GETTY MUSEUM, LOS ANGELES

And he said unto me, Son of man, can these bones live?
And I answered, O Lord God, thou knowest.

—EZEKIEL 37:3

MAGNOLIAS OVERSHADOWED MISERY," observed Frederic Denison, Regimental Chaplain, 3rd Rhode Island Heavy Artillery Regiment, at the "Old Fort Plantation," Beaufort, South Carolina in December, 1861. When federal troops entered the area, the plantation owners were overthrown, after which they fled in defeat. These abandoned, enslaved Americans were not at that time, 1862, declared free people by the federal government. Timothy H. O'Sullivan, preeminent Civil War photographer, visited this war zone from about November 1861 to March 1862 and preserved in one picture the largest group of enslaved Americans to be photographed at one time. The purpose of this picture-taking is not known. These enslaved Americans seem to stand in a wake of light emerging from the darkness of shadows. Stark slave quarters are behind them; they are winged by a trinity of trees. The old, the maimed, the boy, the girl, the woman, the man, they stand not as victims but as bewildered survivors of an American tragedy.

(*following page*)

HENRY P. MOORE
American, 1833–1911

Slaves of Rebel General Thomas F. Drayton, Hilton Head, South Carolina, 1862

ALBUMEN PRINT

84.XM.483.25

THE J. PAUL GETTY MUSEUM, LOS ANGELES

THIS COMPOSITION CHRONICLES A TRANSITION between two worlds, slave America and free America. Standing, sitting, with burdened heads and downcast eyes, in various styles of dress—all are slaves, in the process of being made free people by the federal government. When the federal troops occupied the lands that the slave owners fled, the abandoned slaves were kept intact to maintain the land for harvest. The women cover their heads, a custom imposed on female slaves, and sit in lower position than the men; one woman stands alone, possibly the head female in this grouping.

All of the men are on a higher elevation, but the white soldier is in control, standing in the front, shifted to the right, as though overseer or master. The tallest man, the Negro in the center with his arms akimbo was probably a slave driver. Historical accounts suggest that blacks serving in this capacity were more hated than the former master and were ostracized by the still-enslaved Americans.

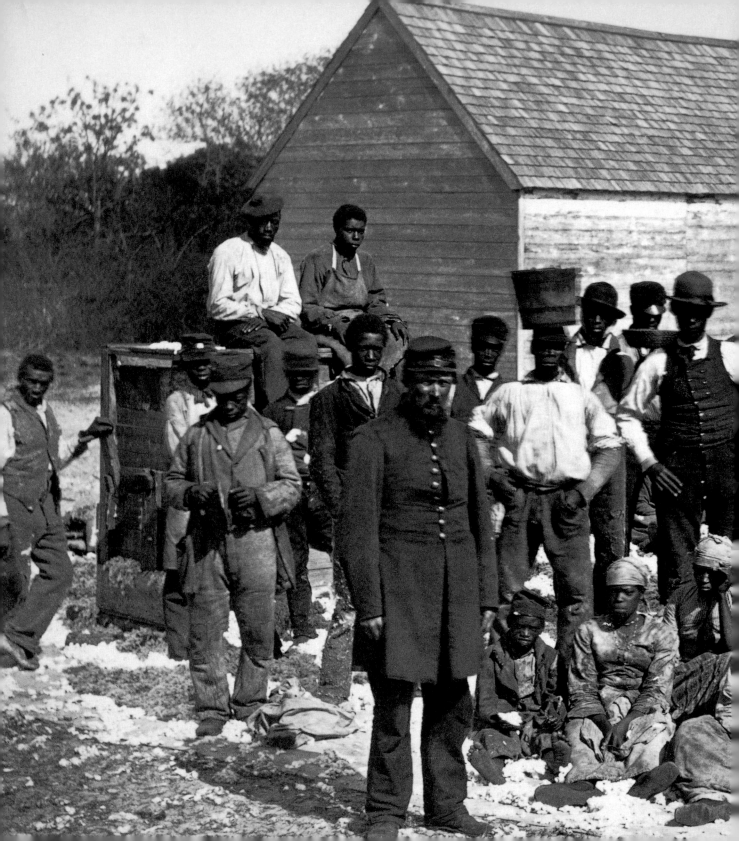

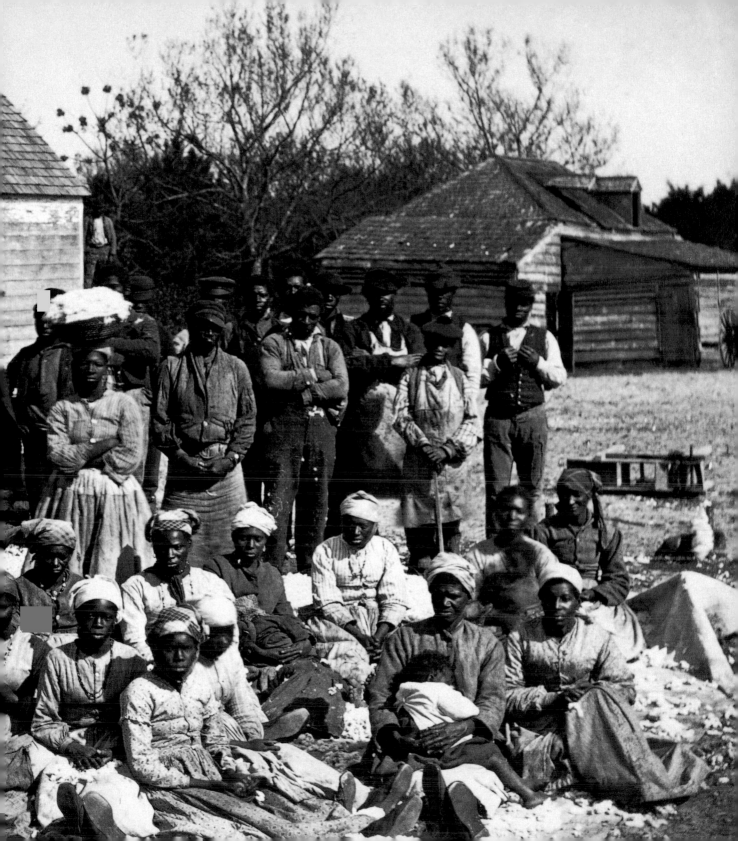

UNKNOWN MAKER

American School

A Zouave Tribesman, ca. 1850

SIXTH-PLATE DAGUERREOTYPE

JACKIE NAPOLEAN WILSON COLLECTION

DURING THE 1830s, ZOUAVE TRIBESMEN IN North Africa were left in charge of a colonial garrison by the French. Their administration was so successful that they were incorporated into the French Army and became its most notable colonial soldiers. This man wears a Zouave uniform of the same type worn by other European armies, such as those who fought in the Crimean War and was worn by the Papal Zouaves in defense of the Papal States in 1860. In America both the North and South during the Civil War admired this exotic uniform style. Early in the Civil War, President Lincoln's friend Colonel Elmer E. Ellsworth toured the United States with his regiment of Fire Zouaves, creating a sensation wherever they performed their acrobatic feats. This could be a photograph of one of them.

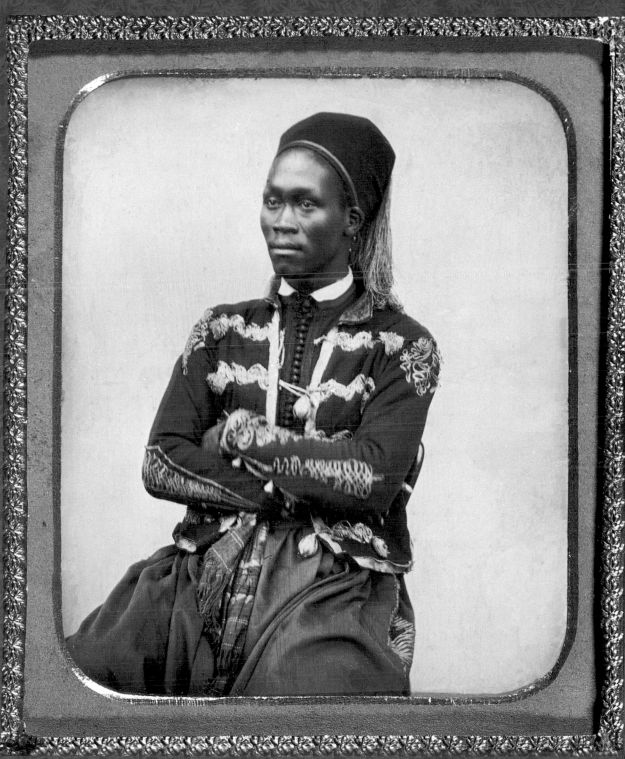

UNKNOWN MAKER

American School

A Full Company of Blue Coats in Winter Quarters with Contraband, ca. 1861–65

HALF-PLATE TINTYPE

JACKIE NAPOLEAN WILSON COLLECTION

T HE CAUSE OF THE CIVIL WAR IS SHOWN front and center here: a young "contraband," a Negro slave who, during the Civil War, escaped to or was brought within the Union lines. African-Americans were not permitted to enlist in the Union Army until 1863. This young contraband is in uniform and was adopted as a harbinger of good luck. He likely had never been far from the confines of the plantation, but he knew that there were non-slaveholding Southerners caught up in the vigilance of patrolling for runaways. His home and all around him held the threat of his being caught, punished, and reenslaved. And, though these men stand as liberators, for African-Americans there was still the lingering quest for equality.

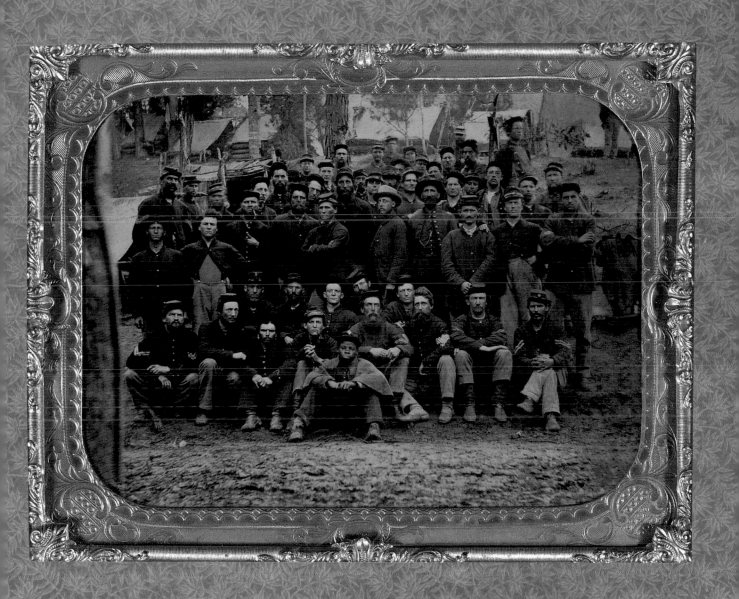

UNKNOWN MAKER

American School

Contraband Teamster, ca. 1861

QUARTER-PLATE TINTYPE

JACKIE NAPOLEAN WILSON COLLECTION

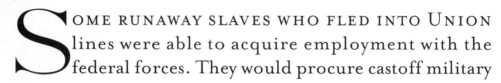

SOME RUNAWAY SLAVES WHO FLED INTO UNION lines were able to acquire employment with the federal forces. They would procure castoff military clothing, but they were not soldiers. This tall, confident-looking man was likely a contraband field hand who became a laborer. He looks to be one who was hired as a teamster who loaded, hauled, and unloaded heavy goods, artillery, and equipment for the Union forces. We might wonder, for whom did this fugitive have this picture made?

This young African-American man surely experienced many conflicting thoughts. For example, if the North won the war and millions of slaves were freed, how could he locate and assist his relatives? For the contraband the issue was more complex: How could he survive outside the plantation system, where one's needs were provided for at least in some minimal fashion?

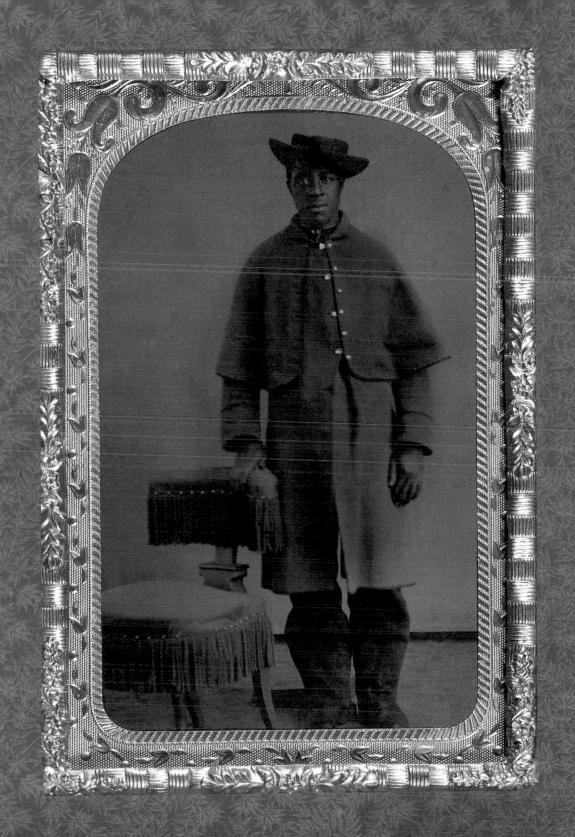

UNKNOWN MAKER

American School

Contraband Carpenter, ca. 1861–65

SIXTH-PLATE TINTYPE

JACKIE NAPOLEAN WILSON COLLECTION

SOME RUNAWAY SLAVES WHO FLED INTO UNION lines had skills and occupations acquired on the plantations. This man holds a saw, which is the symbol of his trade. It was probably the first time that this carpenter had received pay for his work, for he could not afford any clothes better than the simple vest and under-size hat that he wore to the photographer's studio. Early photographs of African-Americans suggest that once they earned enough money to buy fine clothes, they dressed to emulate white society, the only model of society they had.

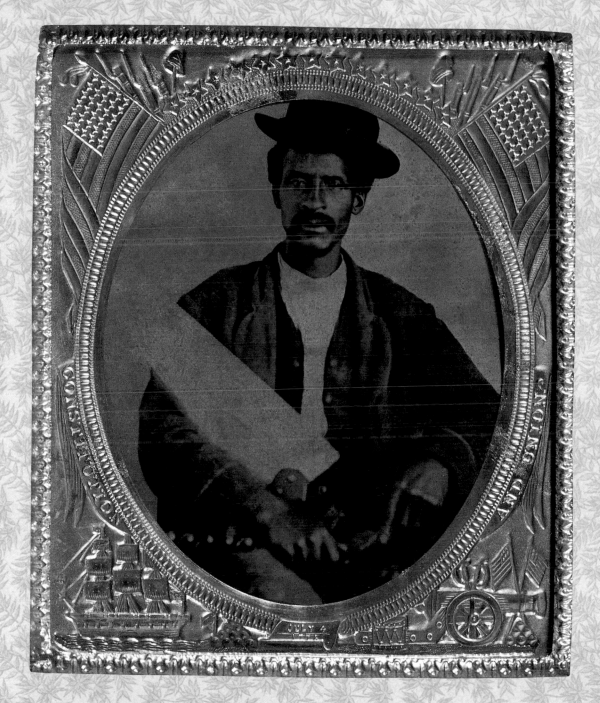

UNKNOWN MAKER

American School

Contraband with French Cap, ca. 1861–65

SIXTH-PLATE TINTYPE

JACKIE NAPOLEAN WILSON COLLECTION

THIS MAN WEARS THE CLOTHES SIMILAR TO A court jester, but he is not a fool. His face seems to show a façade many Negroes had to portray—humble.

Though he wears mostly military garb, it is too ragged for an official soldier. Military officials from foreign lands came to this country to observe the American Civil War. This man's cap has the patriotic colors of the French Revolution, blue, white, and red: *Liberté, Egalité, Fraternité.*

Is his inner spirit concealed in the face of this contraband? Was he threatened with being sent back into slavery? He was not treated as an equal by the look of him in this picture. Would comments be made about his race? How did he feel about his flight to freedom to a war camp? How could he sense the outcome of this adventure and excitement? How did he react to serving whites who wanted to kill other whites knowing that his race—his presence—was one of the causes of the conflict? If freedom were to come, how did he cope with the thought of locating relatives sold long ago? Where was one to look? Would he walk? And where was one to go? How would he survive? This was probably the first time this man had been away from the plantation; when this photograph was taken, he did not know the outcome of this struggle of a nation in the face of armed conflict.

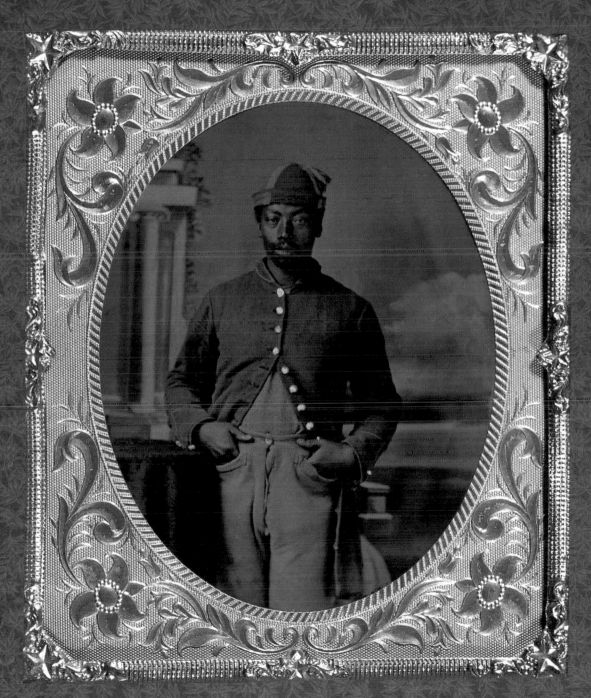

UNKNOWN MAKER

American School

Civil War Soldier, Patriotic Backdrop, ca. 1863–65

SIXTH-PLATE TINTYPE

JACKIE NAPOLEAN WILSON COLLECTION

THREE COMPONENTS OF LOVE FOR ONE'S country are shown here. We see his body in uniform, the painted and variegated patriotic camp-life military backdrop, and the seriousness of resolve in his face. One would hardly know that a photographer's stand is behind this man to keep him in position, an assist he does not need.

In the quest for freedom, this photograph shows that the Negro man, contraband and free, came to the defense of the Republic from both sides of the Mason-Dixon line. African-American soldiers who enlisted were proud of their uniforms. They often used part of their small pay allowance to commission portraits from itinerant photographers who traveled in wagons and set up shop in tents near the encampments. Never before did soldiers, facing death, have an opportunity to send their pictures back home to loved ones. Some no doubt died before their pictures got home.

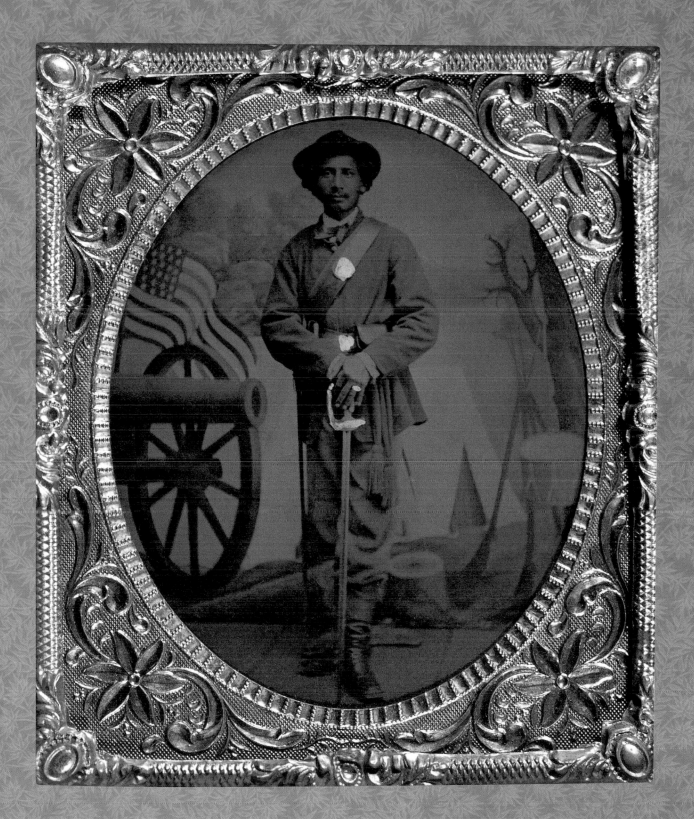

UNKNOWN MAKER

American School

Negro Civil War Soldier and Contraband, ca. 1863–65

SIXTH-PLATE TINTYPE

JACKIE NAPOLEAN WILSON COLLECTION

THIS TINTYPE ILLUSTRATES PROFOUNDLY that the Negro soldier knew that he was at war to free his race. Rare indeed is a photograph with an African-American soldier positioned with a contraband, both having pistol in hand. There is symbolism in the barefoot runaway slave seated on the floor: He is not yet equal to the African-American soldier, who was very likely born free. The soldier was part of the chain of events that would lead to freedom for his people.

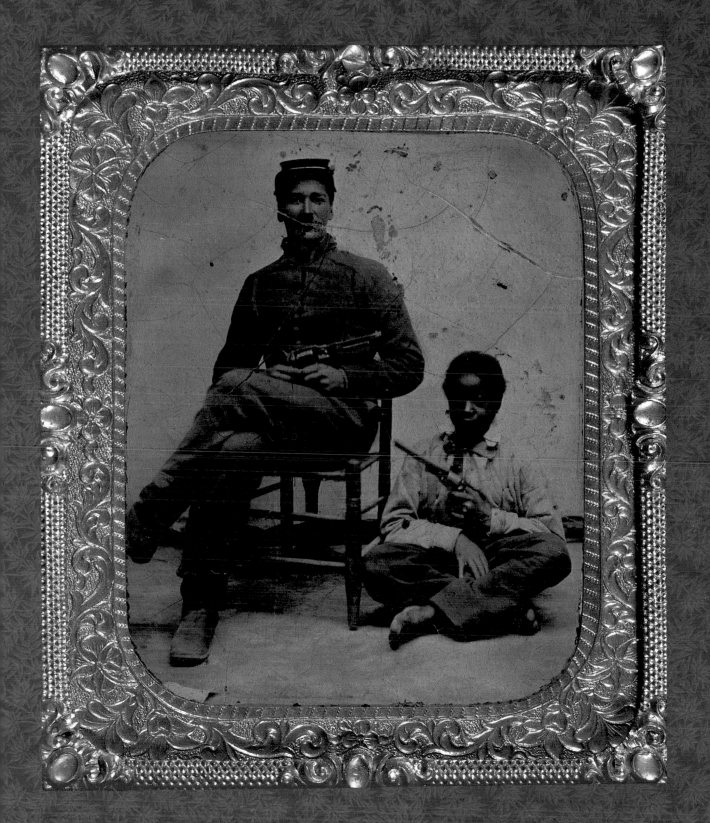

UNKNOWN MAKER

American School

Soldier and Companion, 1863–65

QUARTER-PLATE TINTYPE

JACKIE NAPOLEAN WILSON COLLECTION

NEARLY 180,000 AFRICAN-AMERICANS resisted the Confederacy as Union soldiers during the Civil War. Blacks were not allowed to serve in the Army until 1863. In that year, Frederick Douglass exhorted blacks, in his "Men of Color to Arms!", to "smite with death the power that would bury the government and your liberty in the same hopeless grave." This soldier likely saw the carnage of war and while on furlough was hurried to the photographer by his bright-eyed companion.

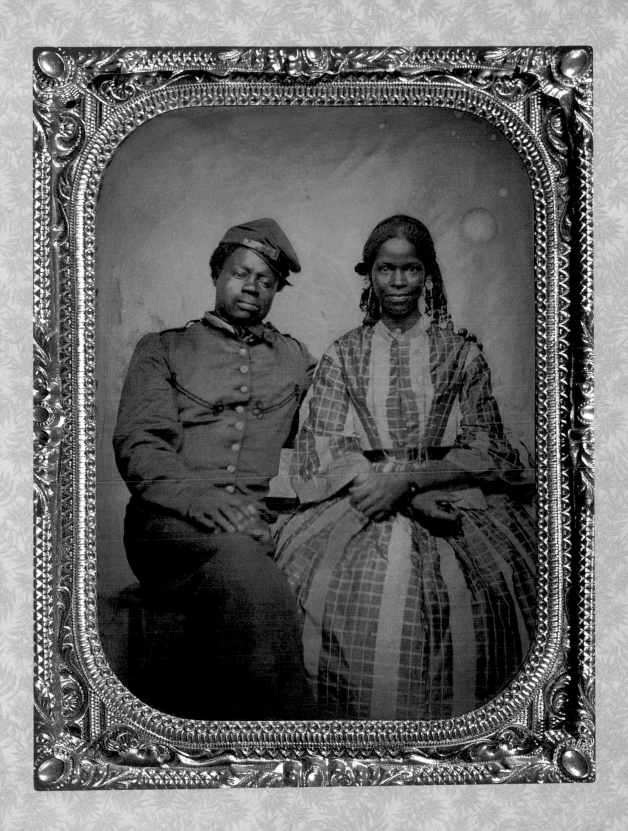

UNKNOWN MAKER

American School

Philadelphia Minister, ca. 1860

SIXTH-PLATE AMBROTYPE

JACKIE NAPOLEAN WILSON COLLECTION

IN THIS IMAGE, A MINISTER EXUDES THE strength of his people. The formality of his clothes are reminiscent of the Fathers of the Nation, and his forthright stance links a people to the founding of this nation, for slave and free, we were there. And in this round-visaged gentleman, in his face and in his clothes, we see that we are Americans interwoven in the fiber of the nation, never to be disengaged, because we were always there.

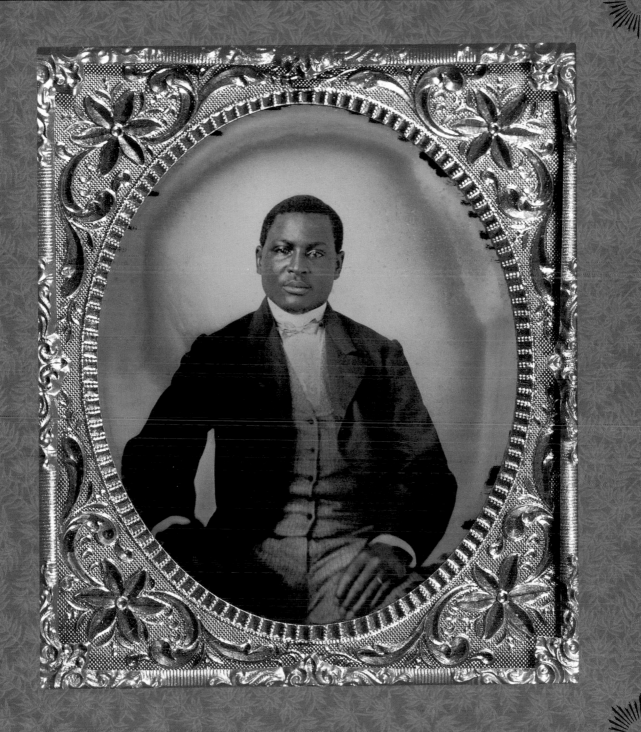

UNKNOWN MAKER

American School

The Departure, ca. 1861–65

HALF-PLATE TINTYPE

JACKIE NAPOLEAN WILSON COLLECTION

THE NAME OF ABRAHAM LINCOLN INSPIRES reverence in anyone whose ancestors were slaves, and no likeness is more prized than his to the collector

of photographs of the Civil War epoch. What I see on this plate is Abraham Lincoln in entourage: the only known photograph of the Great Emancipator in the company of a person of the African race—a young hospital orderly standing under his shadow at an encampment. They may be standing on a battlefield on Virginia soil, at Fredericksburg, at the Falmouth encampment in April 1863, in front of a large hospital tent surrounded by the president's private secretaries John Hay and John Nicolay, along with "French Mary," a vivandière who braved thirteen battles. Two spent

artillery shankle shells are on the ground. The military ambulance in the foreground may have been the wagon Lincoln rode in. He risked his life by venturing so close to the battle lines, and his presence in such a vulnerable situation is in keeping with precedent. Though there is no documentation to this tintype, every time I see his face, this is the man who led us to the demise of American slavery and with that the beginning of the struggle for complete freedom for a people, who before were caretakers for other people and not for themselves.

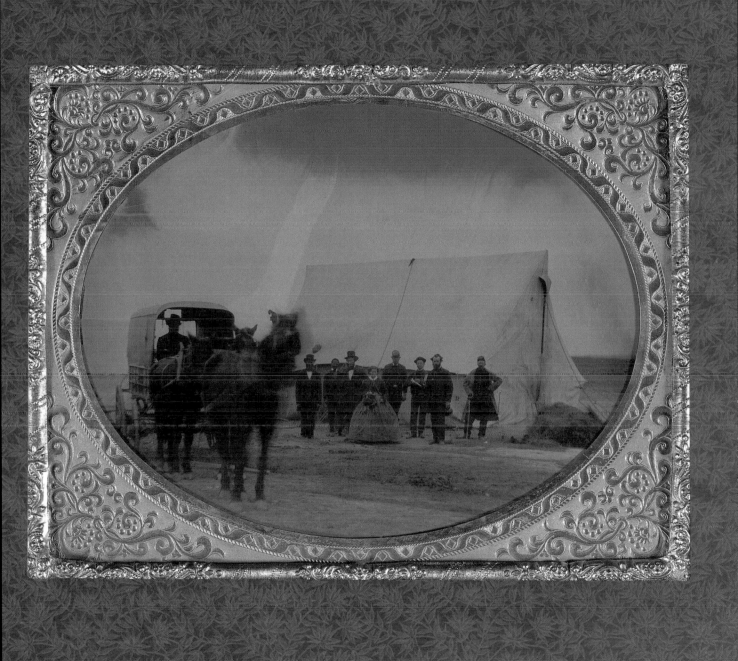

UNKNOWN MAKER

American School

Portrait of a Mother and Child ("Madonna"), ca. 1860

SIXTH-PLATE TINTYPE

JACKIE NAPOLEAN WILSON COLLECTION

THIS TINTYPE, DATING FROM THE EARLY 1860s, is one of the most remarkable female portraits in all of nineteenth-century photography. The mother's expression is beatific and a spiritual aura fills the image. This "Madonna" is a small miracle. The strong-featured woman is dressed in garments that are of high quality but not luxurious. She holds her child nestled against her bosom in the nursing position that recalls old master paintings of the "Madonna and Child." A delicate cross is resting on her right ribbon. She displays her child and the wedding band on her left hand with equal pride. We see in this woman an emblem of the end of the slave society and beginning of a new era based on freedoms guaranteed by the Thirteenth, Fourteenth, and Fifteenth Amendments to the Constitution of the United States that were the chief legislative accomplishments of the Civil War. She is symbolic of the rebirth of a nation and of a people once held in bondage.

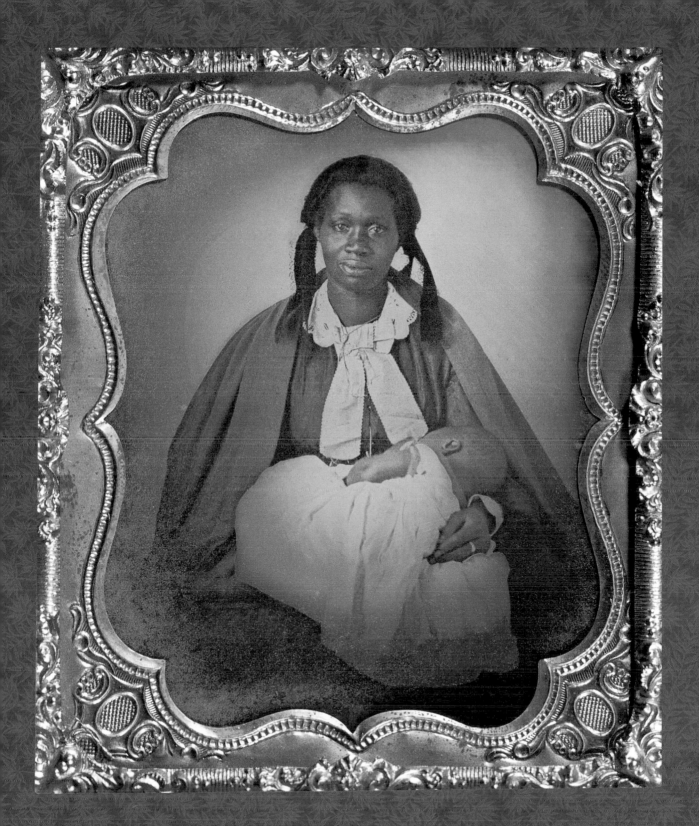

IT IS A MYSTERY HOW FROM "A CLOUD OF WITNESSES" THESE ANCESTORS came to me. Weston Naef, Curator of Photographs from the J. Paul Getty Museum, told me in my home that these images "must have come on the wings of angels." ❧ My mentor William (Bill) Sayles Doan of Fort Dodge, Iowa, once told me that there was a need for a "gleaner," a searcher for lost images of people whose destinies have not come down to us. Years ago Bill Doan and I arrived at the title *Hidden Witness* for my collection of photographs of African-Americans made before and during the Civil War, but we knew of no image that could be singularly viewed as the

ACKNOWLEDGMENTS

Hidden Witness. When Weston Naef invited me to the Getty, in its study room, I discovered the *Hidden Witness,* and for this I am eternally grateful to him. ❧ It is with heartfelt appreciation that I chronicle those who brought these discoveries to the attention of the public: Ellen Sharp, the Detroit Institute of Arts; *Michigan Citizen; Michigan Chronicle;* Susan Agar, *Detroit Free Press;* Itabari Njeri, *Los Angeles Times;* Judith Endelman and Nikki Shakoor of the Henry Ford Museum and Greenfield Village; *Newsweek* magazine; and Weston Naef of The J. Paul Getty Museum, whose vision made the *Hidden Witness* exhibition a milestone in photographic history. ❧ I will always remember Nathan Brandt, former editor of *American Heritage,* who visited my home in 1987 and said at the door, "I came to see the *Madonna.*" I responded, "You mean the *Mother and Child.*" And he said again, "I have come to see the *Madonna. She is a Madonna.*" ❧ A personal discovery must be credited to my late brother's widow, Rosa Wilson, who assisted my pre-exhibition research and found recorded evidence of my lineage to the American Civil War through my paternal grandfather, Jack Jackson Wilson. Up until that time, I had very few remnants of family history, except that my mother had told me that he was born a slave and lived to be 107 years old. Rosa also discovered that my great-uncle James Henderson was a state representative and radical Republican from South Carolina who voted on the ratification of the Fourteenth Amendment to the Constitution of the United States. ❧ There are others whose words and acts of kindness remain with me always: Gordon Baldwin, Assistant Curator at the Getty Museum, who provided me the wisdom that as the collector I have the right to speak to what is in my holdings; The Getty Museum for contributing the reproductions that are in this book, and a special thanks to the entire Department of Photographs at the Getty for their valuable assistance; R. H. "Shell" Hensleigh of the Detroit Institute of Arts whose fine photographic reproduction work provided the framework that led to the *Hidden Witness* exhibition; The Detroit Institute of Arts was gracious at providing the condition reports, and I thank conservator Valerie Baas for the services she rendered. ❧ There are many photographic collectors and dealers whose paths I have crossed while acquiring these images, but I only note a very few: William B. Becker, Howard McManus, and Gary Vroegindewey, who were the sources of masterpieces that loom large in my collection. ❧ Ruth J. Moffett, Mrs. Martin, and James Lewis saw this book from afar. This book would not have been possible were it not for Marcus Walker, who selflessly encouraged me from my first acquisition. Francis Scheurer was a friend and a father to me and encouraged me always until he died at eighty-seven years, a year after the *Hidden Witness* exhibition. My sister Janet Peoples was the dearest to me, and did not live to see this book in print, but her words resonate throughout it, especially words she said about the *Hidden Witness.* ❧ To Jennie Dunham, my literary agent, I say our hope has turned real. ❧ There are so very many individuals from years gone by to whom I would like to pay tribute. Though not mentioned here, you know who you are.